MODERN WORLD LEADERS

Gordon Brown

MODERN WORLD LEADERS

Michelle Bachelet

Ban Ki-moon

Tony Blair

Gordon Brown

George W. Bush

Felipe Calderón

Hugo Chávez

Jacques Chirac

Hu Jintao

Hamid Karzai

Ali Khamenei

Kim Jong Il

Thabo Mbeki

Angela Merkel

Hosni Mubarak

Pervez Musharraf

Ehud Olmert

Pope Benedict XVI

Pope John Paul II

Roh Moo Hyun

Vladimir Putin

Nicolas Sarkozy

The Saudi Royal Family

Ariel Sharon

Viktor Yushchenko

Modern World Leaders

Gordon Brown

Alan Allport, Ph.D.

CHELSEA HOUSE
PUBLISHERS
An imprint of Infobase Publishing

Chelsea House
An imprint of Infobase Publishing
132 West 31st Street
New York, NY 10001

Library of Congress Cataloging-in-Publication Data
Allport, Alan, 1970-
  Gordon Brown / by Alan Allport.
    p. cm. — (Modern world leaders)
  Includes bibliographical references and index.
  ISBN 978-1-60413-080-5 (acid-free paper)
1. Brown, Gordon, 1951—Juvenile literature. 2. Prime ministers—Great Britain—Biography—Juvenile literature. 3. Great Britain—Politics and government—1997—Juvenile literature. 4. Politicians—Great Britain—Biography—Juvenile literature. 5. Labour Party (Great Britain)—Biography—Juvenile literature. I. Title.
  DA591.B76A55 2009
  941.086092—dc22
  [B]   2008026565

TABLE OF CONTENTS

On Leadership

Leadership, it may be said, is really what makes the world go round. Love no doubt smoothes the passage; but love is a private transaction between consenting adults. Leadership is a public transaction with history. The idea of leadership affirms the capacity of individuals to move, inspire, and mobilize masses of people so that they act together in pursuit of an end. Sometimes leadership serves good purposes, sometimes bad; but whether the end is benign or evil, great leaders are those men and women who leave their personal stamp on history.

Now, the very concept of leadership implies the proposition that individuals can make a difference. This proposition has never been universally accepted. From classical times to the present day, eminent thinkers have regarded individuals as no more than the agents and pawns of larger forces, whether the gods and goddesses of the ancient world or, in the modern era, race, class, nation, the dialectic, the will of the people, the spirit of the times, history itself. Against such forces, the individual dwindles into insignificance.

So contends the thesis of historical determinism. Tolstoy's great novel *War and Peace* offers a famous statement of the case. Why, Tolstoy asked, did millions of men in the Napoleonic Wars, denying their human feelings and their common sense, move back and forth across Europe slaughtering their fellows? "The war," Tolstoy answered, "was bound to happen simply because it was bound to happen." All prior history determined it. As for leaders, they, Tolstoy said, "are but the labels that serve to give a name to an end and, like labels, they have the least possible

6

connection with the event." The greater the leader, "the more conspicuous the inevitability and the predestination of every act he commits." The leader, said Tolstoy, is "the slave of history."

Determinism takes many forms. Marxism is the determinism of class. Nazism the determinism of race. But the idea of men and women as the slaves of history runs athwart the deepest human instincts. Rigid determinism abolishes the idea of human freedom—the assumption of free choice that underlies every move we make, every word we speak, every thought we think. It abolishes the idea of human responsibility, since it is manifestly unfair to reward or punish people for actions that are by definition beyond their control. No one can live consistently by any deterministic creed. The Marxist states prove this themselves by their extreme susceptibility to the cult of leadership.

More than that, history refutes the idea that individuals make no difference. In December 1931, a British politician crossing Fifth Avenue in New York City between 76th and 77th streets around 10:30 P.M. looked in the wrong direction and was knocked down by an automobile—a moment, he later recalled, of a man aghast, a world aglare: "I do not understand why I was not broken like an eggshell or squashed like a gooseberry." Fourteen months later an American politician, sitting in an open car in Miami, Florida, was fired on by an assassin; the man beside him was hit. Those who believe that individuals make no difference to history might well ponder whether the next two decades would have been the same had Mario Constasino's car killed Winston Churchill in 1931 and Giuseppe Zangara's bullet killed Franklin Roosevelt in 1933. Suppose, in addition, that Lenin had died of typhus in Siberia in 1895 and that Hitler had been killed on the western front in 1916. What would the twentieth century have looked like now?

For better or for worse, individuals do make a difference. "The notion that a people can run itself and its affairs anonymously," wrote the philosopher William James, "is now well known to be the silliest of absurdities. Mankind does nothing save through initiatives on the part of inventors, great or small, and imitation by the rest of us—these are the sole factors in human progress. Individuals of genius show the way, and set the patterns, which common people then adopt and follow."

Leadership, James suggests, means leadership in thought as well as in action. In the long run, leaders in thought may well make the greater difference to the world. "The ideas of economists and political philosophers, both when they are right and when they are wrong," wrote John Maynard Keynes, "are more powerful than is commonly understood. Indeed the world is ruled by little else. Practical men, who believe themselves to be quite exempt from any intellectual influences, are usually the slaves of some defunct economist.... The power of vested interests is vastly exaggerated compared with the gradual encroachment of ideas."

But, as Woodrow Wilson once said, "Those only are leaders of men, in the general eye, who lead in action.... It is at their hands that new thought gets its translation into the crude language of deeds." Leaders in thought often invent in solitude and obscurity, leaving to later generations the tasks of imitation. Leaders in action—the leaders portrayed in this series—have to be effective in their own time.

And they cannot be effective by themselves. They must act in response to the rhythms of their age. Their genius must be adapted, in a phrase from William James, "to the receptivities of the moment." Leaders are useless without followers. "There goes the mob," said the French politician, hearing a clamor in the streets. "I am their leader. I must follow them." Great leaders turn the inchoate emotions of the mob to purposes of their own. They seize on the opportunities of their time, the hopes, fears, frustrations, crises, potentialities. They succeed when events have prepared the way for them, when the community is awaiting to be aroused, when they can provide the clarifying and organizing ideas. Leadership completes the circuit between the individual and the mass and thereby alters history.

It may alter history for better or for worse. Leaders have been responsible for the most extravagant follies and most monstrous crimes that have beset suffering humanity. They have also been vital in such gains as humanity has made in individual freedom, religious and racial tolerance, social justice, and respect for human rights.

There is no sure way to tell in advance who is going to lead for good and who for evil. But a glance at the gallery of men and women in MODERN WORLD LEADERS suggests some useful tests.

One test is this: Do leaders lead by force or by persuasion? By command or by consent? Through most of history leadership was exercised by the divine right of authority. The duty of followers was to defer and to obey. "Theirs not to reason why/Theirs but to do and die." On occasion, as with the so-called enlightened despots of the eighteenth century in Europe, absolutist leadership was animated by humane purposes. More often, absolutism nourished the passion for domination, land, gold, and conquest and resulted in tyranny.

The great revolution of modern times has been the revolution of equality. "Perhaps no form of government," wrote the British historian James Bryce in his study of the United States, *The American Commonwealth*, "needs great leaders so much as democracy." The idea that all people should be equal in their legal condition has undermined the old structure of authority, hierarchy, and deference. The revolution of equality has had two contrary effects on the nature of leadership. For equality, as Alexis de Tocqueville pointed out in his great study *Democracy in America*, might mean equality in servitude as well as equality in freedom.

"I know of only two methods of establishing equality in the political world," Tocqueville wrote. "Rights must be given to every citizen, or none at all to anyone ... save one, who is the master of all." There was no middle ground "between the sovereignty of all and the absolute power of one man." In his astonishing prediction of twentieth-century totalitarian dictatorship, Tocqueville explained how the revolution of equality could lead to the *Führerprinzip* and more terrible absolutism than the world had ever known.

But when rights are given to every citizen and the sovereignty of all is established, the problem of leadership takes a new form, becomes more exacting than ever before. It is easy to issue commands and enforce them by the rope and the stake, the concentration camp and the *gulag*. It is much harder to use argument and achievement to overcome opposition and win consent. The Founding Fathers of the United States understood the difficulty. They believed that history had given them the opportunity to decide, as Alexander Hamilton wrote in the first Federalist Paper, whether men are indeed capable of basing government on "reflection and choice, or whether they are forever destined to depend ... on accident and force."

Government by reflection and choice called for a new style of leadership and a new quality of followership. It required leaders to be responsive to popular concerns, and it required followers to be active and informed participants in the process. Democracy does not eliminate emotion from politics; sometimes it fosters demagoguery; but it is confident that, as the greatest of democratic leaders put it, you cannot fool all of the people all of the time. It measures leadership by results and retires those who overreach or falter or fail.

It is true that in the long run despots are measured by results too. But they can postpone the day of judgment, sometimes indefinitely, and in the meantime they can do infinite harm. It is also true that democracy is no guarantee of virtue and intelligence in government, for the voice of the people is not necessarily the voice of God. But democracy, by assuring the right of opposition, offers built-in resistance to the evils inherent in absolutism. As the theologian Reinhold Niebuhr summed it up, "Man's capacity for justice makes democracy possible, but man's inclination to justice makes democracy necessary."

A second test for leadership is the end for which power is sought. When leaders have as their goal the supremacy of a master race or the promotion of totalitarian revolution or the acquisition and exploitation of colonies or the protection of greed and privilege or the preservation of personal power, it is likely that their leadership will do little to advance the cause of humanity. When their goal is the abolition of slavery, the liberation of women, the enlargement of opportunity for the poor and powerless, the extension of equal rights to racial minorities, the defense of the freedoms of expression and opposition, it is likely that their leadership will increase the sum of human liberty and welfare.

Leaders have done great harm to the world. They have also conferred great benefits. You will find both sorts in this series. Even "good" leaders must be regarded with a certain wariness. Leaders are not demigods; they put on their trousers one leg after another just like ordinary mortals. No leader is infallible, and every leader needs to be reminded of this at regular intervals. Irreverence irritates leaders but is their salvation. Unquestioning submission corrupts leaders and demeans followers. Making a cult of a leader is always a mistake. Fortunately hero worship generates its own antidote. "Every hero," said Emerson, "becomes a bore at last."

The single benefit the great leaders confer is to embolden the rest of us to live according to our own best selves, to be active, insistent, and resolute in affirming our own sense of things. For great leaders attest to the reality of human freedom against the supposed inevitabilities of history. And they attest to the wisdom and power that may lie within the most unlikely of us, which is why Abraham Lincoln remains the supreme example of great leadership. A great leader, said Emerson, exhibits new possibilities to all humanity. "We feed on genius . . . . Great men exist that there may be greater men."

Great leaders, in short, justify themselves by emancipating and empowering their followers. So humanity struggles to master its destiny, remembering with Alexis de Tocqueville: "It is true that around every man a fatal circle is traced beyond which he cannot pass; but within the wide verge of that circle he is powerful and free; as it is with man, so with communities." ●

A Deal
over Dinner

AT ABOUT 10 MINUTES TO EIGHT ON THE EVENING OF TUESDAY, MAY 31,
1994, two men arrived by taxi at the Granita restaurant in north
London's fashionable Islington district. They entered and made
their way to table 13 at the back of the restaurant, where a third
man was waiting for them. After a course of appetizers, one of
the new arrivals, a political consultant named Ed Balls, made
his excuses and left. The two men who remained, old friends
turned bitter rivals, sized each other up. Tony Blair and Gordon
Brown had known each other for more than a decade. Blair
was the British Labour Party's parliamentary spokesmen on
law and order; Brown was the party's spokesman on economic
affairs. They had entered the House of Commons at the same
time, had shared the same office, and had traveled together
extensively. To others in the party, they had been known as "the
twins." For years, both had worked passionately to reorganize
and repackage "New Labour," as it was becoming known, after

the party's four bruising defeats at the polls by the opposing Conservative Party. Each man greatly admired the intelligence, drive, and ambition of the other. Now, for the first time, shocking circumstances had brought them into direct conflict.

Three weeks earlier, the Labour Party's leader, John Smith, had died of a sudden heart attack at the age of 55. Smith had risen to Labour's top post in 1992. It had been taken for granted that he would lead the party into the next general election, which was expected to take place in 1996 or 1997. (In Great Britain, the dates of national elections are not fixed in advance as they are in the United States.) Moreover, Smith was widely tipped to win. Britain was undergoing a deep economic recession, and the Conservative Party, under Prime Minister John Major, was imploding in a series of increasingly ugly battles about membership in the European Union (EU). It looked as if the Conservatives' long dominance, which had begun in 1979 with the election of Margaret Thatcher as prime minister, might be over at last. Now Smith's tragic death had brought a new uncertainty to the upcoming contest. Who would head the Labour Party in its best chance for political office in a generation?

Neither Blair nor Brown made any secret of the fact that each coveted the job. In the weeks after Smith's death, public proclamations of sadness had been accompanied, behind the scenes, by a discreet but furious whispering campaign among Labour's members of Parliament (MPs). Which of the two should be chosen leader, the whisperers asked. Although both men had strong partisan support, the odds slightly favored Blair. Each man had a realistic chance of seizing the prize. The fear in Labour's ranks, however, was that prolonged infighting between the Blair and Brown camps would give the Conservatives some much-needed breathing space and might allow Major to rally his own exhausted and divided party. No Labour supporter wanted to live through a fifth general-election defeat in a row. In an attempt to avoid that nightmare

During a crisis of leadership in Britain's Labour party, it was decided that Tony Blair *(right)*, without opposition from his rival Gordon Brown *(left)*, would run as the organization's official representative in upcoming elections. The politicians agreed that as long as Brown stepped aside for Blair to serve as prime minister, Brown would later succeed Blair as the next leader of Great Britain.

scenario, Blair had secretly invited his rival to the Granita for a one-to-one discussion. Blair wanted, it is said, to cut a deal.

What took place during that dinner has never been adequately explained. Both politicians have refused to discuss the matter. The most persistent rumor is that Blair made Brown an offer: If Brown agreed not to contest the party-leadership election, he would be given responsibility, in a future Labour administration, for the direction of economic and social policy. This in effect, would put Brown in charge of all the important aspects of domestic government. Meanwhile, Blair, as prime minister, would adopt a hands-off policy on purely internal matters. He would concern himself more with Britain's foreign affairs. Moreover—and this is even more speculative—it is rumored that Blair said that after two terms in office—in other words, after 10 years—he would step down to allow Brown to succeed to the top job.

The dinner broke up; no definite agreement is known to have been made. What we do know, however, is that the following afternoon, Peter Mandelson—at the time, one of Labour's most influential "managers" and the man widely believed to be responsible for the Granita meeting—arranged for Blair and Brown to pose, smiling, for television cameras in front of Parliament's iconic clock, Big Ben. Brown, it was announced, had decided not to contest the election. He would support his old friend. "I believe Tony Blair will lead us to election victory," Brown wrote the same day: "I'm standing aside for a united fight." Mandelson and other Labour campaigners were delighted. The party's approval ratings soared and remained sky high for years to come. Later, in private, Brown appeared to take the decision very differently, however. When a TV reporter suggested that the real reason he had declined to fight was because he knew he would lose, Brown, watching, is reported to have screamed and cursed at the television set and kicked his office furniture in anger. When Blair went on to win the leadership election with a less-than-overwhelming 57 percent of the vote, Brown's frustration at what might have been is said to have reached new heights. Had Brown been swindled?

Thirteen years later, after three historic election wins, Prime Minister Tony Blair did stand down in favor of Brown. For a decade, Brown had been Britain's chancellor of the exchequer, the nation's senior economic statesman. Whether his appointment to this post was the result of the "deal" forged in Islington back in 1994 will, perhaps, never be known. Nor will we ever know what might have happened had Brown declined Blair's offer and possibly gone on to succeed John Smith that year. Would Labour have won in 1997? If it had, with Brown

After years of squabbling and political power plays, Tony Blair *(above)* resigned as prime minister in 2007 to allow Brown to take his place. Despite party affiliation, the two had little in common and were often at odds.

THE RELATIONSHIP BETWEEN BROWN AND BLAIR IS ONE OF THE MOST FASCINATING PARTNERSHIP-RIVALRIES IN BRITISH POLITICS IN THE PAST CENTURY.

at the helm, how "New" would New Labour have been? Under Brown, would the party have been dogged by the allegations of "sleaze" and "spin-control" that characterized Blair's early years in office? Would Brown, always more cautious than Blair on transatlantic matters, have agreed to take part in the United States-led invasion of Iraq in 2003? It was Blair's decision to do so that chipped away so much of his once rock-solid public popularity.

Gordon Brown became prime minister of the United Kingdom in 2007. The next general election probably will be held in about 2010. Between now and then the world will find out what sort of administration Prime Minister Brown has chosen to pursue. His array of options, however, have, to a large extent, been predetermined by the man whom he supported so stoically, if ambivalently, for a decade. The relationship between Brown and Blair is one of the most fascinating partnership-rivalries in British politics in the past century. The contrast between the very different styles, ideas, and personalities of the two men has come to define the course of recent British public life. This book will trace Brown's lengthy and often turbulent journey to Number 10 Downing Street. It will also reflect on what sort of distinctive stamp Brown may try to put on domestic and international affairs now that his longtime friend and competitor has at last left the political stage. Blair's Britain has passed. What does Brown's Britain look like?

2

Brown's Early Years

JAMES GORDON BROWN (HE EVENTUALLY ABANDONED HIS FIRST NAME) WAS born on February 20, 1951, in Govan, a suburb of the Scottish city of Glasgow. He was the second son of John Ebenezer and Jessie Elizabeth, or "Bunty," Brown. John Brown was a minister in the Scottish Presbyterian Church. When Gordon was three years old, his father took up residency in the town of Kirkcaldy, a large port in the region of Fife, just across the Firth estuary from Scotland's capital, Edinburgh. It was in the manse, or minister's house, attached to St. Brycedale's Church in Kirkcaldy that Gordon Brown grew up.

Kirkcaldy had been a prosperous place during the heady years of the late nineteenth century. The *Lang Toun* ("Long Town"), as the Scots call it, was famous for its linoleum and linen factories, and its bustling harbor was filled with ships shuttling to Edinburgh and Dundee with the Fife coal that powered the Scottish industrial revolution. Kirkcaldy also boasted one of Scotland's most celebrated thinkers. Economist and philosopher Adam Smith was born in Kirkcaldy and lived there until he was fifteen. In 1776, Smith published *The Wealth of Nations*. In that work he proposed that an "invisible hand" guided the collective behavior of individual buyers and sellers in the marketplace and that a nation's economy worked to the best advantage of all when it was allowed to operate according to the laws of supply and demand, with only minimal government interference. *The Wealth of Nations* was a groundbreaking work in the development of economic thought, and it helped to establish the intellectual foundations of modern free-market capitalism. During the 1800s, the wisdom of such thought appeared to be borne out by the success, in Scotland and elsewhere, of thousands of manufacturing centers such as Kirkcaldy.

By the time that John Brown arrived in Kirkcaldy, however, the town's luck had taken a turn for the worse. Shifts in global trading patterns after World War II had reduced the demand for Scottish textiles and coal, and Kirkcaldy's once-packed harbor was empty of ships. The history of the *Lang Toun's* rise and fall taught a harsh lesson in the fickleness of the free market. The invisible hand could grant prosperity, but it also could snatch it away. Many members of John Brown's congregation were the victims of Kirkcaldy's misfortune. They were poor and jobless, bewildered and demoralized by circumstances largely out of their control. Growing up in the depressed Scottish "rust-belt," young Gordon Brown had a schooling in the darker side of industrial capitalism that had profound influence on his values later in life.

Gordon's father became a successful and well-respected member of the Kirkcaldy community. One of his colleagues later described him as "an able preacher and a superb pastor, distinguished by selfless concern for those committed to his care." John Brown was an old-fashioned and fiercely reverent Presbyterian. At times this made life at the manse a little austere

"BEING BROUGHT UP AS THE SON OF A MINISTER MADE ME AWARE OF COMMUNITY RESPONSIBILITIES THAT ANY DECENT SOCIETY OUGHT TO ACCEPT."

—Gordon Brown

and even dull for his children. Prayers were said regularly before mealtimes, and attendance at church twice on Sundays was mandatory for the whole family. The commandment to "honor the Sabbath Day" was interpreted so rigorously that Sunday newspapers could not be read until Monday.

John Brown was not a pious humbug or a hypocrite, however. He took his Christian responsibilities very seriously. Everyone in Kirkcaldy knew that they would always find a welcome at the Browns' door. This sense of duty was impressed on Gordon and his brothers, John and Andrew. On one occasion, Gordon's parents came home to find their son sitting at the kitchen table with Kirkcaldy's most notorious burglar. He had come to the manse, Gordon explained, simply for something to eat. The visit went smoothly enough, but the Browns had a few anxious moments afterward as they checked that the family silver was still in place.

What effect did life as a "son of the manse" have on Gordon Brown the politician? Journalists and biographers have spent a great deal of time pondering this question. It is interesting to note that Margaret Thatcher, a major figure in twentieth-century British politics, also grew up in a strictly religious, middle-class household in a small provincial town. Was there something about the atmosphere of their very similar homes that propelled both Thatcher and Brown toward careers in public life? In Brown's case, he does not seem to have retained much of the Presbyterian Church's overt Christian faith. There are very few references to God or religion in his later writings or speeches. Throughout his career, however, Gordon Brown always has maintained that his childhood at the manse was important to his moral and intellectual development. "Being brought up as the son of a minister made me aware of community responsibilities that any decent society ought to accept," he has said. Whatever Brown's attitude may be toward matters of faith, he certainly was influenced by the Presbyterian belief in the duties of social responsibility.

If Brown's upbringing did prepare him for life as a statesman, it was not initially clear that he was interested in pursuing such a life. As a child, his overwhelming passion was sport. He was a talented tennis and rugby player, and at school he took part in rowing and sprinting. His greatest love of all, however, was soccer. He was good enough to seriously consider a career as a professional soccer player, and he was a devoted supporter of the local team, Raith Rovers. He spent his Saturday afternoons outside the playing ground selling programs to ticket-holders so that he could get free admission at halftime. Brown is still an avid soccer fan, and he prides himself on his knowledge of obscure Scottish soccer statistics. He continues to attend Raith Rovers home games whenever possible, and he takes a personal interest in the team's fortunes: In 2005, when he was still chancellor of the exchequer, Brown assisted in the creation of a locally owned consortium that bought out the club, which had been tottering on the brink of financial collapse. Brown has been known to argue at great length with Rovers' manager John McGlynn about what tactics the team should follow. "Let's come to an agreement," McGlynn is supposed to have told this exasperating fan. "I won't tell you how to manage the country—and you won't tell me how to manage Raith Rovers!"

Young Gordon Brown was pressed to show academic as well as athletic excellence. Scotland has a prestigious education system that is organized quite differently from that of the rest of Great Britain, and the Scottish system regularly produces university candidates of especially high quality. By the time he reached Kirkcaldy High School, Brown was in an experimental fast-track scheme. This placement meant that he was taught alongside boys and girls who were two years older than he was. The youngster did not particularly enjoy this "privilege." He later wrote that it was "ludicrous" for educators to push young people like himself so hard, often making their lives miserable in the process, just to get them into university a couple of years earlier than normal. He considered this an accomplishment of very dubious value, and he remains opposed to such "hothouse" education today.

UNIVERSITY

In 1967, at the age of 16, the fast-tracked Brown joined his brother John at the University of Edinburgh, one of Scotland's four esteemed "ancient" universities. "This is my brother Gordon," John is supposed to have said when introducing his younger sibling to the student newspaper editor: "He's boring but very clever." Gordon quickly settled into university life, excelling both academically and on the sports field. Before his second semester had ended, however, he faced a dreadful and completely unexpected setback. A few weeks after coming to Edinburgh, Brown, always a ferocious athlete, was injured in a rugby match. He was accidentally kicked in the head, and he discovered afterward that his sight was impaired. At the time, he said nothing. He hoped that the problem would go away by itself. After six months, however, it was obvious that his vision was getting worse, not better. He was forced to see a doctor, who diagnosed detached retinas in both eyes. The delay in seeking treatment had worsened the damage.

During the next two years, Brown had four operations on his eyes at Edinburgh Royal Infirmary. Between operations, he had to lie immobile, sometimes for months at a time, in a darkened hospital ward. Unable to read, he later described the process as "a living torture." Worse, its success was only partial.

Gordon Brown entered Edinburgh University *(above)* at an early age and excelled in academics and extracurricular activities. When a rugby accident ended any hope of a professional sports career, Brown began to concentrate on working with the university's Labour Club and the student newspaper. His success and dedication during this time helped shape his political career.

The sight in Brown's right eye was saved, although impaired, but his left went blind completely. Eventually, he had a glass eye put into the socket. This ended any prospect of a career in professional sports. It also changed Brown, both physically and mentally. To this day, his eyesight is poor. When he speaks in Parliament, he needs to have his speeches printed in large type. Because of lost muscle movement on the left side of his face, he began to develop what some people have misinterpreted as a permanent sulky grimace. Although the frown was a medical accident rather than a feature of his personality, Brown returned to university a much more serious young man than he had been before. He was determined, after long hours spent in useless captivity on a hospital bed, not to waste any more precious time. His thoughts were beginning to turn to politics.

This was not a completely new development. Despite his boyhood dreams of soccer stardom, Brown had always been interested in current affairs. When he was 13, Gordon and his brother John began to write and publish a homemade sixpenny newspaper. The brothers produced their paper on a duplicating machine in the manse. Gordon described this publication somewhat grandiloquently as "Scotland's only newspaper sold in aid of African refugees" because the boys donated their small profits to charity. Brown pulled off an impressive scoop when, after writing to NASA, he landed an exclusive interview with astronaut John Glenn, the first American to orbit the Earth. Brown also wrote about British and international politics. His party allegiance already was becoming clear, and he enjoyed arguing about the merits of socialism with his school's conservative librarian. When American president John F. Kennedy was assassinated, in November 1963, Brown took the news particularly badly. "Gordon saw [Kennedy] as the future," recalls one of his then-schoolmates, "and could not believe the future had been so brutally snuffed out. He was shocked and stunned. He kept saying, 'I cannot believe that this has happened.'"

At the University of Edinburgh in 1968, Brown began to put his earlier political interest into practice. In 1969, he joined the Labour Party. In his second year at university, he became chairman of the university Labour club and editor of the student newspaper. As a journalist, Brown unearthed a minor campus scandal in 1970. At the time, South Africa was practicing its racist policy of apartheid, and there was great pressure on academic institutions not to invest or have any financial dealings with the regime in Pretoria. Thanks to a pertinent document leaked to him by a sympathetic staff member, Brown was able to reveal that the University of Edinburgh held investment shares in a number of South African companies. This was something that the university's trustees had vehemently denied in the past. It was the young activist's first brush with celebrity. It also made him some enemies among the university's elite, and he was to pay for it later on.

Brown the university student cut a curious figure. He never paid any attention to his appearance and often looked more like a tramp than a politician-in-waiting. He stamped around Edinburgh in a dirty overcoat with plastic supermarket bags in each hand, stuffed with newspaper clippings, pamphlets, and notes. His time-management skills were hopeless, and he was late to almost every meeting. As bad as his personal grooming was, his housekeeping habits were even worse. The student lodgings (or "digs," as they are known) that he shared with several other undergraduates were renowned as the most untidy in Scotland. According to legend, the apartment once was the subject of a minor break-in. When a police officer inspected the building afterward, he said he had never seen the site of a robbery so badly vandalized. "Really?" said Brown. "It looks pretty normal to me."

Despite his scruffy ways, Brown was a hard worker. He was rarely distracted from the task at hand. Although he adopted the long-haired hippie look of many of his peers, he took little interest in alcohol and none at all in drugs—something that was to spare him a great deal of awkwardness with the press later in life. (In contrast, British politician David Cameron faced an embarrassing scandal after he became Conservative Party leader in 2005: It was revealed that he had been punished for smoking marijuana at school.)

Brown was known for sitting up until the early hours of the morning, tapping away on his typewriter. This did not detract from his personal charm, however. He hosted many student parties, and his friends from university days remember him as highly charismatic. He was not at all the grim-faced workaholic he is sometimes represented as being. "I never understood when you [later] heard about this dour character," says Simon Pia, a radio presenter who was tutored by Brown. "He had a very easy charm. He was a big star and had a natural way with people." Women, according to another friend, "went goggle-eyed" over young Brown: "He had energy, magnetism, and a terrific voice. I saw the power Gordon had to mesmerize people."

One young woman with whom Brown struck up a most unlikely relationship in 1970 was Princess Margarita of Romania. This eldest daughter of the exiled King of Romania was a fellow student at Edinburgh. She became Brown's girlfriend for eight years and acted as a protective "mother hen," trying to sort out his chaotic work schedule and compensate for his limited housekeeping skills. The romance between a would-be socialist politician and a member of Europe's aristocratic elite was never going to be a straightforward one. In the end, however, the relationship appears to have fizzled out not so much because of the couple's differences in background as because of Brown's inability to find time and emotional space for his partner. "It was a very solid and romantic story . . . I never stopped loving him," Margarita later said. "But one day it didn't seem right any more—it was politics, politics, politics, and I needed nurturing."

Although Brown would have a few more girlfriends during the 1970s and early 1980s, his solitary habits made him a difficult match. He spent his leisure time in private and in largely male or naturally solitary pursuits. He watched hour after hour of soccer matches on television and listened to records of such artists as opera star Jessye Norman and crooner Frank Sinatra. Until his surprise marriage in 2000, many of his friends assumed that Brown would remain a bachelor for life.

A START IN POLITICS

In 1972, Brown graduated from Edinburgh with a master of arts degree in history. He earned first-class honors, the highest possible grade. He also decided to stay on and pursue a doctorate in history, examining the development of Labour Party politics in Scotland in the 1920s. Brown received his doctoral degree in 1982, and he subsequently published his research as a book. Brown is, in fact, the only British prime minister ever to be awarded a doctorate on his own merits. Other prime ministers have received honorary degrees as marks of respect for their political achievements. Brown has never highlighted his academic credentials. Britain is a country notoriously suspicious of intellectuals, and it can be politically dangerous for a British politician to appear to be too intelligent. It is clear, however, that Brown has an impressive knowledge of history, political thought, and philosophy. His speeches are sometimes peppered with references to figures such as Voltaire, John Stuart Mill, Charles Darwin, and—perhaps naturally—his fellow Kirkcaldian, Adam Smith.

During Brown's years at the University of Edinburgh, he became better known for his involvement in university politics than for his scholastic accomplishments. The same year that he graduated with his masters degree, Brown launched a bid to be elected rector of the university. The position, chosen every three years by the students and staff, was a largely honorary one that usually was held by an aging dignitary. It did come with one substantive role, however: The rector acted as the convener, or chairman, of the university court, the institution's governing body. This meant that the rector, if he or she chose, could use the position to highlight shortcomings in university administration and generally make life difficult for the vice-chancellor, the university's day-to-day governor. Because Brown had a long history of conflict with the University of Edinburgh that dated back to the South African investment affair, he mischievously relished such an opportunity. He launched a sophisticated

TRUTH REVEALED

Gordon Brown's plan to involve as many students as are intersted in the university's affairs was revealed yesterday when he met national pressmen. Speaking of the blatant need for a better feedback between Court and students and vice versa, he made three specific proposals

✶ He will appoint eight students as Assessors and will invite a member of the non academic staff to represent the technicians, servitors and

cleaners who are as yet unrepresented

✶ He will have a Rectorial Advisory Committee with ▮▮▮▮▮▮ last year's Rector, the Senior President of the S.R.C. and Union Presidents to advise on Court business

✶ He will set up a series of informal working parties on issues like student housing in the centre, communicty action, and university goverment. All students interested will be invited to join in.

Said Brown:"This is the one way we can involve students in the future of the University If more students than before are thinking positively about where we're going, then there is a great change to change the University"

"We will also have general meetings before Court meetings and I hope to write a weekly

STUDENT RECTOR

WHO NEEDS AN OUTSIDER?

The University Court has , on it, two High Court judges, an industrialist, an accountant, a retired civil servant, four Profesoors, a headmaster - even a representative for North Sea Oil. But there are no student members - unless we elect a student Rector next Friday.

WHO IS SIR FREBERICK?

Sir Frederick Catherwood is an accountant, an industrialist a retired civil servant, a lecturer - all positions already represented on the Court - and an Oxbridge graduate who now lives in London.

GORDON BROWN FOR STUDENT RECTOR

Gordon Brown is a first year history postgradute who has just completed an honours degree in arts here. He has been in Edinburgh for five years and in that time edited"Student chaired the Publications Board and been a co editor of "Alternative Edinburgh". He is a student, in contact with students, and will be in Edinburgh at all times. He also has the support of almost all sections of student opinion

WHO NEEDS AN OUTSIDER? ONLY A STUDENT WILL DO

GORDON BROWN

black jack

Deputy Secretary to the University, ▮▮▮▮▮ is reported to be worried at the possibility of having' another student as Rector. ▮▮▮▮▮ who prides himself in his knowledge of grass roots ordinary middle of the road students is understood to have been telling the few students he knows to vote for ▮▮▮▮▮ to keep out Gordon

Strange. ▮▮▮▮▮ is also Deputy Returning Officer for the election and impartial. He is also the well known secretary to the Court whose interrretation of what has gone on at Court meetings has been more than once questioned by ▮▮▮▮▮

Gordon Brown gained a reputation for muckraking after exposing Edinburgh University's investments in South African companies. His continued push for change drove him to run for rector of the university, a position that allowed him to blow the whistle on some of the university's less attractive practices. *Above*, a flyer advertising Brown's campaign for student rector.

THE VICE-CHANCELLOR ALLEGEDLY CONNIVED TO ENSURE THAT, DESPITE HIS QUALIFICATIONS, BROWN DID NOT OBTAIN A PERMANENT TEACHING POSITION AT THE UNIVERSITY.

political campaign across the campus to drum up support, and he won the election. The vice-chancellor, Sir Michael Swann, was a staunch Conservative and had been the subject of Brown's journalistic criticisms in the past. Swann refused to accept the voters' decision and tried to have Brown removed. Unperturbed, Brown took his case to the Court of Session, the city of Edinburgh's high court, and won. It did not hurt that the chancellor of the university was the Duke of Edinburgh, who also happened to be Brown's girlfriend Margarita's godfather. The duke was willing to put in a quiet word of support for the young upstart.

Rector Brown wasted no chance to annoy Vice-Chancellor Swann. Among other things, Brown demanded the publication of an itemized list of the expenses and allowances paid to senior university officials. Swann did have his revenge, however. When Brown's term as rector expired in 1975, the vice-chancellor allegedly connived to ensure that, despite his qualifications, Brown did not obtain a permanent teaching position at the university. Brown had no choice but to seek employment elsewhere. The following year, he became a lecturer in politics at Glasgow College of Technology, a school now known as Glasgow Caledonian University. Following this, in 1980, he moved back into journalism as the current affairs editor for Scottish Television (STV).

During these years, Brown also was becoming more and more involved in Scottish Labour Party affairs. In the February 1974 general election, he played a major role in getting his colleague Robin Cook elected as a member of parliament for Edinburgh Central. Cook later became one of Brown's most important political colleagues. In October 1974, there was yet another general election, and Brown launched a bid to be nominated as Labour Party candidate for a neighboring parliamentary constituency. He was unsuccessful, but the seed of ambition had been sown.

In 1975, he helped to raise his profile within the party ranks by editing a book of essays, *The Red Paper on Scotland*. Although the *Red Paper* sold only a few thousand copies, it proved to be highly influential among party activists. To read Brown's foreword to the book more than 30 years later is to see clearly that Brown has taken a long political journey since his student days The *Red Paper* is a scorching work of unapologetic socialism. The authors of the essays collected and edited by Gordon Brown demand state planning, nationalization of industries, a fully planned economy, and the destruction of the ruling class—sentiments that are very hard to imagine coming from the leader of New Labour today. Not all of Brown's old policies have been abandoned, however. It is clear that from the outset, he was at best lukewarm about federal devolution— that is, the granting of a greater measure of home rule—for Scotland. Devolution was a fashionable cause in the 1970s, and, as such, was one to which an up-and-coming party member might have been tempted to pander.

In 1979, the year that Margaret Thatcher became prime minister, Brown finally won Labour Party backing to contest a parliamentary seat in the general election. He stood for the Edinburgh South constituency but lost to the local Conservative candidate, Michael Ancram. Ancram was another University of Edinburgh graduate who was entering parliament for the first time. He later became deputy leader of the Conservative Party. Brown's bid was quite impressive, however: He fell barely 2,000 votes short of first place. Perhaps more importantly, he established himself as a credible candidate, one whom the Labour Party presumably would consider for a more winnable seat the next time around. As Brown awaited the next general election, he took time out from his duties at Scottish Television to coauthor a book with Robin Cook. *Scotland: The Real Divide* was a survey of problems of poverty and inequality—an early attack on the political doctrine that already was coming to be known as "Thatcherism."

In June 1983, Prime Minister Thatcher called a new general election. Brown's moment had arrived. He was nominated for Dunfermline East, a new constituency that adjoined Kirkcaldy, and he won with a rousing 11,301 majority. A seat in the House of Commons now was his. On the evening of the day of the victory, Jonathan Wills, a journalist and close friend of Brown's, showed up at Brown's house to congratulate the new member of parliament. Wills found Brown slumped in an armchair in a darkened room. "There's a beer over there. Sit down and shut up," Brown barked at him. "I've never seen anyone as depressed in my life," Wills later recalled. The reason for Brown's unhappiness was not difficult to determine. Labour may have triumphed in Dunfermline East, but elsewhere in Britain, the party had been trounced. The Conservative prime minister was returning to power with an enhanced majority of 37 seats and a mandate for even more sweeping Thatcherism. Brown was about to join the ranks of a depleted and sadly disillusioned parliamentary Labour Party.

CHAPTER

3
Thatcherism and New Labour

GORDON BROWN WAS NOT ALONE IN LAMENTING THE RESULT OF THE 1983 general election. Labour supporters everywhere groaned as they watched the steady disintegration of their hopes that June night. In its worst performance in more than 60 years, Labour lost more than 51 parliamentary seats and managed to gain barely one quarter of the popular vote. The party almost was pushed into third place, behind the Social Democratic Party and Liberal Party. Many commentators argued that Labour was finished as a leading force in British politics. Few among Brown's beleaguered colleagues could have dared to guess that, 13 years later, the story would be completely reversed, and that Labour would enter power with more MPs than any political party in British history. To understand this dramatic change in Labour's fortunes during the 1990s—a change in which Gordon Brown played no small part—one needs to take a step back for a moment to consider the profound consequences of Margaret Thatcher's arrival in British politics.

"THE SICK MAN OF EUROPE"

"By the end of the 1970s, Britain was in a mess." It is hard to disagree with this assessment by Conservative politician Kenneth Baker. The country that had emerged victorious from two world wars and that at one time had been the industrial powerhouse of the world seemed to have lost its way. Unemployment was worsening rapidly even as the prices of household goods were rising and the purchasing power of wages was falling in an unpleasant combination known as "stagflation." During the 1970s, Britain was rocked by a series of bitter labor disputes, by racially motivated violence in the inner cities, and by terrorist attacks. A succession of Conservative and Labour governments tried, without success, to bring the country back under control, but the nation appeared rudderless. Internationally, battered Britannia became known as the "sick man of Europe." "Who Governs Britain?" asked Conservative Prime Minister Edward Heath in February 1974, as he announced a general election campaign to shore up his ailing administration. Heath got the electorate's answer a few weeks later, when they threw him out of office: maybe no one, and certainly not you.

Some of Britain's maladies in the 1970s simply were part of a much wider problem that had spread across the capitalist Western world. The United States had run up such enormous debts during the long Vietnam War that finally ended in 1975 that the American dollar had lost much of its value, and the American economy was sinking into recession. Because the United States was the hub of the international economy, its weakness inevitably caused its trading partners, in turn, to falter. Additionally, in 1973, the Yom Kippur War broke out between Israel and the neighboring Arab states of Egypt, Syria, and Iraq. Although Israel won, the oil-rich Arab nations of the Organization of the Petroleum Exporting Countries (OPEC)

Great Britain suffered from a series of incidents in the 1970s, including a large coalminer's strike, violent conflicts in Ireland, and fuel shortages. During the premiership of Edward Heath, who as Conservative Party leader led the country from 1970 to 1974, things went from bad to worse. Heath failed to settle domestic issues, causing Great Britain to be labeled "the sick man of Europe."

decided to punish America and Western Europe for their support of the Israeli government by dramatically raising the price of crude oil. Because the industrial nations of the West were by this time absolutely dependent on foreign oil for their

NOBODY IN BRITAIN SEEMED TO WANT TO WORK ANYMORE.

day-to-day functioning, the result was a stunning blow to their economies. In Britain, fuel shortages forced the government to introduce rationing at gas stations. The so-called "Oil Shock" had inflationary effects that continued throughout the decade of the 1970s.

Britain also was in the midst of a breakdown in industrial relations. Strike actions by the leading trade unions had grown increasingly disruptive during the 1960s. As union leaders were emboldened by their successes in winning wage claims, so, too, did union members became more militant and the unions' demands more ambitious. The most dominant and radical union was the National Union of Mineworkers (NUM). Coal was second only to oil as the fuel on which the British economy ran, and the government owned and operated the coal mines. Because of this, the NUM knew that it could put a stranglehold on the government anytime it chose, and it was increasingly willing to exercise that power. At the height of the oil crisis, NUM leaders launched a campaign for a wholesale pay increase. In 1974, when this request was refused, the miners went out on strike. The strike brought coal production to a halt. Heath's government had to introduce a three-day work-week across British industry, extending the weekend by two days to conserve dwindling coal stocks. Electrical blackouts became commonplace as power stations ran out of fuel. In the end, the government surrendered and settled with the miners.

The NUM's success encouraged other unions to take a more militant approach. Railroad workers, road-haulage drivers, public-works employees, and healthcare staff also took part in strike actions. Union leaders argued that their members needed wage hikes to compensate for the constant rises in prices. The price rises were real enough, but the overall effect of the strikes was to slowly strangle the British economy. Nobody in Britain seemed to want to work any more.

As the economy staggered, the country also suffered from serious social unrest. Tension grew between the white majority and the multiracial communities that had settled in Britain's cities in the years that followed World War II, a period during which immigration from the Caribbean and South Asia increased. White-racist political parties such as the National Front gained votes. Minority youths accused the police of petty intimidation and harassment. Such things served to widen the divide between the nonwhite communities and the British authorities. In 1976, minority youths' suspicions boiled over into action. At the Notting Hill Carnival in west London, rioting and running street battles broke out between black teenagers and police.

At the same time, the conflict in Northern Ireland between Catholics and Protestants—the so-called "Troubles"—spilled over onto the British mainland. The Irish Republican Army (IRA) began a campaign of bombings in London and other major cities to intimidate the British government into withdrawing from the Irish north. In 1974, the worst year, 24 people were killed in four bomb attacks in the English cities of Birmingham and Guildford. British democracy itself appeared to be in fragile shape.

THATCHER AND THATCHERISM

Into this chaos stepped Margaret Thatcher. She was the unlikeliest of persons to command, let alone dominate and revolutionize, the British Conservative Party. The Tories, as the Conservatives are known, previously had chosen most of their leaders from a close-knit aristocratic elite. Britain's great wartime prime minister, Winston Churchill was the grandson of a duke. Harold Macmillan, a Tory who served as prime minister from 1957 to 1963, appointed 35 family members to his own government. Margaret Thatcher came from a completely different world. She was the daughter of a respectable but modest shopkeeper in the Midlands town of Grantham, Lincolnshire.

Like Gordon Brown's family, Thatcher's was devoutly religious; her father was a Methodist lay preacher. Also like the Browns, the Thatchers were hard working and civic-minded. Margaret Thatcher obtained a scholarship to Oxford to study chemistry; it was at university that she became interested in Conservative politics. In 1959, Thatcher obtained a seat in the House of Commons; throughout the early 1960s, she worked her way quietly but thoroughly through a series of minor posts in successive government administrations. The idea of a woman, let alone a Tory woman, taking an active role in politics still was something of a novelty at the time; Thatcher was encouraged in her career by senior Conservatives who liked the touch of modernity and glamour that she brought to their rather staid and musty ranks. In 1970, she entered the cabinet as Edward Heath's secretary of state for education. In that post, Thatcher became a nationally known figure for the first time; and when Heath's government collapsed ignominiously in February 1974, she decided to make a bid for the party leadership. To everyone's surprise (except, perhaps, her own), she was elected leader the following year.

Whatever else might be said about her, Thatcher did have a refreshingly clear view of what was wrong with Britain. The problem, as she saw it, lay not with the oil crisis or any other particular event; these were just symptoms of a much deeper malaise. Britain, she believed, had taken a fundamentally wrong course after World War II. In 1945, Winston Churchill's wartime government had been replaced by a Labour administration led by Clement Attlee. During the next six years, in a series of sweeping measures, Attlee and his colleagues transformed the old free-market British economy. The Labour government nationalized—that is, brought understate ownership—large sectors of industry and production such as the railroads and the coal mines. The Labour government also created a free, universal healthcare system, the National Health Service (NHS), and a series of national insurance-payment schemes for unemployment, sickness, and old age—a system known collectively as the welfare state. Attlee lost power in 1951, but when the Conservatives took office, they saw how popular the reforms had become. They decided not to repeal them. During the 1950s and 1960s, a broad consensus emerged between the two major parties that the country should be run according to common principles: The government should take a leading hand in the day-to-day running of the economy, and the welfare safety net should be expanded to eliminate the social evils of poverty and want.

Thatcher regarded this consensus as sheer folly. To her mind, clumsy state mismanagement and dependency on government handouts had sapped Britain's entrepreneurial spirit. To pay for the increasingly expensive NHS and the broader welfare state, both the Tories and Labour had been forced to raise income taxes. As Thatcher saw it, this discouraged any incentive to create wealth. Unproductive jobs were propped up artificially by the government, thereby making British goods more expensive to produce and hopelessly uncompetitive overseas. The only answer, in her opinion, was a rollback of the state. Taxes must be reduced, Thatcher believed, and government spending on welfare cut back accordingly. The free market had to be allowed to operate without interference, so that Adam Smith's "invisible hand" could act to the benefit of all. If jobs were lost in the short-term, so be it. It was a small price to pay if the long-term health of the economy improved.

Only in matters of law and order did Thatcher see an enhanced role for the government. Lawlessness, she believed, was rising because irresponsible individuals had learned to regard society with contempt. From now on, criminals would be punished severely. Terrorists would be weeded out ruthlessly. Internationally, the vehemently anti-communist "Iron Lady" (as the Soviets came to call her) called for a hard line against the USSR.

In May 1979, after a dismal winter of strikes, the Labour government under James Callaghan collapsed, and Thatcher was elected prime minister, with a small majority. She now had a chance to put her beliefs into practice.

LABOUR'S RESPONSE TO THATCHERISM

The Labour Party's initial reaction to Thatcher's election was a mixture of hostility and condescension. To Labourites, her free-market mantra seemed hopelessly out of date; in any case, they thought, she would be bound to bow to the realities of the nationalized, welfare-state economy in the end. Other would-be revolutionaries had come and gone from British politics without accomplishing anything. The more complacent of Labour's supporters were in for a shock. Thatcher slashed state spending, raised interest rates to reduce inflation, and sharply reduced the rate of income tax, shifting the source of government revenue to sales tax, instead—a measure that her opponents said stole from the poor to give to the rich. Initially, the results were worrying. Inflation remained high, and unemployment began to rise rapidly as manufacturing jobs were lost. Soon, 3.6 million people were out of work.

By the beginning of 1982, Thatcher's popularity was at a record low, and Labour confidently expected to return to power at the next election. The Iron Lady received a respite in the unlikeliest of ways, however. In May 1982, Argentina invaded the Falkland Islands, a British territory in the South Atlantic, off the coast of South America. Argentina claimed the small archipelago as its own territory. The Falklands had a tiny population and were of little economic value, but Thatcher regarded the attack as an intolerable affront to international law. She sent a task force of troops, ships, and aircraft to retake the islands. Against considerable odds, the British forces succeeded, and the Falklands were liberated by June. For what seemed like the first time in decades, Britain had taken on a difficult challenge and won. Thatcher was a national hero.

The "Falklands Factor" certainly played a role in Thatcher's reelection in 1983, but there was more to it than that. After four years of pain, the British economy was starting to respond positively to Thatcher's free-market reforms. Perhaps more importantly, the Labour opposition was in turmoil. The party was divided between moderates such as Dennis Healey and more radical leftists such as Tony Benn, the figurehead of the "Bennites", who believed that the answer to Thatcherism was a return to even more uncompromising socialism. Party leader Michael Foot, who had taken over after James Callaghan's defeat, clearly sympathized with the radical left. In 1981, a group of centrist Labour leaders, disgusted with what they regarded as their party's turn to fantasy politics, left Labour to form the Social Democratic Party (SDP). For the 1983 election, Labour unveiled its most extreme left-wing program ever. The party promised, among other things, to withdraw from the North Atlantic Treaty Organization (NATO), to abolish nuclear weapons, and to enact sweeping new government spending bills. The result was the party's worst showing in an election since World War I. The 1983 manifesto, groaned one Labour leader, was "the longest suicide note in history."

Such was the grim condition of Labour when Gordon Brown joined it in the House of Commons in 1983. Despite the obvious disappointment he must have felt at his party's poor showing, however, the young MP did not seem to have altered his views very much from those he held when he edited and wrote his foreword to *The Red Paper* back in 1975. Brown's politics were still within Labour's left-wing tradition. He complained bitterly about the loss of manufacturing jobs in Scotland caused by Thatcher's cutbacks, and he advocated a return to higher taxes and a higher spending economy. In 1984, the NUM called a national strike to protest pit closures in the coal industry. Brown, whose constituency contained several coal mines, fully supported the action. The strike lasted a year. This was no rerun of 1974, however. Thatcher had prepared for the confrontation, and the mineworkers, defeated, eventually drifted back to work. The failure of the NUM strike permanently broke the back of trade-union power in Britain.

Things now were changing within the Labour ranks. After his 1983 election defeat, Michael Foot stepped aside to make way for a new leader, Neil Kinnock. Kinnock's reputation as a firebrand left-winger initially made him popular among the militant Bennites. His most important characteristic turned out to be his pragmatism, however. Kinnock had no doubt that the party's disastrous performance in 1983 was the result of its failure to connect with the electorate. He publicly distanced himself from the most extreme factions within Labour and sought to rebrand the party as moderate, centrist, and (most of all) sensible. In 1986, he brought in television producer Peter Mandelson to be Labour's new director of communications. Mandelson, an accomplished practitioner of "spin," or public relations, gave Labour a symbolic redecorating. The party's old symbol, the revolutionary red flag, was replaced with a gentler red rose. In 1987, when Thatcher called a new general election, Mandelson stage-managed Labour's campaign and won praise for his imaginative advertising. Despite his efforts, however, Labour still lost soundly that year. Clearly, rebranding was not going to be enough.

For Gordon Brown, the 1987 defeat was a breakthrough, both in terms of career prospects and in terms of political tactics. Two years earlier, he had become a junior member of the government. He worked alongside his friend and fellow Scot, John Smith, on trade and industry affairs. Now, Brown was appointed as the youngest member of the "shadow cabinet," the senior group of Labour MPs in loyal opposition to the government. As shadow chief secretary to the treasury, Brown was Labour's second most important spokesman on economic matters. He remained his chaotic old self, however. He turned up at shadow cabinet meetings late and with ragged papers and notes bursting out of his overstuffed bags. He sometimes

Brown proved to be an impressive critic of Thatcher's government

arranged business dinners with colleagues only to forget to book a table or to show up to discover that the restaurant was closed.

Brown proved to be an impressive critic of Thatcher's government, however. He was particularly good at obtaining official documents that embarrassed the Conservatives; he disclosed these "leaks" to the press and spoke of them in his own weekly newspaper column. His superiors took notice. "He's going to be the leader of the Labour Party one day," said Kinnock. The Conservatives also were beginning to notice the upstart Scot. "He's becoming a little dangerous," said Thatcher's deputy prime minister, William Whitelaw, to one of his colleagues.

At the same time, Brown was starting to reconsider some of his old political assumptions. Labour's performance in the 1987 election was somewhat less awful than it had been in 1983, but the Conservatives still were comfortably ahead. It was becoming clear that many aspects of Thatcher's reforms no longer could be reversed. Most state-owned industries had been sold into private hands, and there was no enthusiasm to renationalize them. Thatcher's income-tax cuts were popular. Additionally, she had removed the bureaucratic red tape that had controlled financial dealing in the City of London, thereby creating a boom of prosperity in the southeast of England. True, parts of Britain remained unconverted by the Thatcher Revolution, especially areas such as the north of England, Wales, and Brown's own Scotland—areas in which the job losses of the early Thatcher years had hit hardest. Labour could not win a national election based on support in these regions alone, however.

In the summer of 1988, Brown traveled to America. He spent three weeks at Harvard University, poring over books and thinking hard about Labour's problems. The party, he decided, had made only cosmetic changes. Mandelson had improved the packaging, but the party continued to offer the same old solutions. The voters were not fooled. To win back the electorate, it would be necessary for Labour to accept some of Thatcher's policies. In public, of course, Brown continued to hammer away at the Conservatives. In 1989, he published another book, *Where There's Greed: Margaret Thatcher and the Betrayal of Britain's Future.* The following year, he mocked Thatcher as "an ageing leader . . . sounding too old to care, determined to stay on at any price."

In the end, Thatcher did fall. She was brought down, not by Labour, but by her own closest colleagues. By 1987, Thatcher had completed most of what she had set out to do but showed no interest in stepping down. As there are no term limits in British politics, other Conservatives began to fear that she would stay on for years more, despite the fact that the voters were showing signs of becoming increasingly tired of her. Continual victory had bred overconfidence and arrogance. When, despite the warnings of her advisers, Thatcher tried to introduce an unpopular property-tax reform, the result was a damaging fiasco. The prime minister appeared to listen to no one any more.

Under Conservative Party rules, any Tory Member of Parliament could make an annual challenge for the leadership of the party if he or she so chose. In November 1990, Michael Heseltine, a disgruntled former cabinet member turned rival, announced that he would take on Thatcher. Thatcher won the opening round of voting, but she failed to get a sufficiently decisive victory to end the contest. A second round would have to take place. Initially, Thatcher wanted to continue, but her ministers bluntly informed her that it was time to depart. The Conservatives remained in power; the question was who would lead them. After a series of bids, John Major, a largely unknown Tory who only recently had become chancellor of the exchequer, emerged as the front-runner and was voted in. Thatcher was gone. What would her legacy be?

THE JOHN MAJOR YEARS AND THE BIRTH OF NEW LABOUR

John Major had a colorful family history. He was the son of a former music-hall performer who had run a business that made and sold garden gnomes. John Major himself had a rather bland personality, however, and he did not come across at first as a very impressive politician. With Major at the Tory helm, Labour's leaders felt that they had an excellent chance of winning the next election—an election that probably would come in 1992. In preparation, Brown and John Smith embarked on what they called the "prawn cocktail circuit." They met with senior financiers in the City of London to try to persuade them that Labour would not reverse Thatcher's reforms. It was clear that John Smith, in particular, had little taste for this sort of cozying-up. He remained, despite his cheerful demeanor, a die-hard socialist.

When the election campaign began, Smith was honest, though imprudent, enough to admit to the public that if Labour returned to power, the party would raise income taxes. "You've lost us the election," wailed Brown afterward. Predictably, the Conservatives mercilessly exploited what they called Labour's "double whammy" of high taxes and higher prices. In the event, in 1992, Major's Tories lost 40 seats but still managed a narrow victory. Labour had closed the gap considerably, but the effect of a fourth straight defeat in a general election cannot be over exaggerated. Labour politicians such as Brown had spent their entire careers in opposition. Now the Tories would remain in power for another five years. Was Labour capable of winning an election any longer?

One thing was clear: Kinnock would have to go. Brown made discreet enquiries as to whether he would be a realistic challenger for the leadership. Tony Blair, by this time one of Labour's other rising stars, urged Brown to run. In the end,

Margaret Thatcher *(above right)* was prime minister of Great Britain when Gordon Brown joined the Labour Party. Fragmented and self-destructive, the Labour Party could not compete against Thatcher's popularity at the time, in spite of the mixed results of her economic and social reforms. John Major *(above left)* took over for Thatcher after she resigned in her third term as prime minister.

Brown declined, however; he did not want to challenge John Smith. "I felt I owed a debt of gratitude," Brown later said. In private, Blair was less generous: "He chickened out." Smith took over and promoted Brown to shadow chancellor of the exchequer. Brown was now the second most powerful man in the party.

The leaders of Labour saw one comforting sign of success in 1992: Across the Atlantic, Democrat William Jefferson Clinton won election as U.S. president, defeating the one-term Republican incumbent, George H.W. Bush. Brown and Blair flew to Washington in January 1993 to talk to Clinton's advisory team. The former Arkansas governor had promoted himself as a believer in the so-called "Third Way" approach to politics. This was a centrist philosophy, one that adopted the best aspects of both socialism and free-market capitalism while rejecting their extremes. The two Labour men saw the Third Way as a means of reformulating their party's policies to suit post-Thatcher Britain.

Back home, Brown began to speak more about the creation of wealth than about its redistribution. He downplayed the old language of haves and have-nots and instead promoted wider access to opportunity for those who had talent. "We do not tax for its own sake," he insisted, "we are not against wealth." Some more traditional members of the party, including (it is said) John Smith, were unconvinced by talk of a Third Way. It was, complained one union leader, all "mischief-making and about personal ambition" on the part of Brown and Blair. Whether Smith would have accommodated himself to the new approach will never be known, however. In May 1994, he died. Three weeks later, the Granita deal was struck. On July 21, Blair became party leader, with Brown as his loyal deputy.

Blair wasted no time in thoroughly reshaping what he referred to as New Labour. The party constitution was amended to remove an old commitment to the nationalization of the economy. The trade unions, which had always had official standing and voting rights within the Labour Party, lost much of their power to influence the procedure for electing the party leader. Meanwhile, John Major's government was visibly falling apart. Margaret Thatcher's closest supporters had never forgiven the "traitors" within the Conservative Party who had toppled her in 1990. Several of those traitorous Tories now were Major's colleagues. The former prime minister herself made no secret of the fact that she regarded her successor as a disappointment.

In September 1992, on a humiliating day known as Black Wednesday, Major's chancellor of the exchequer, Norman Lamont, had been forced to reverse his financial policy completely after a futile attempt to prop up the value of the British pound. The withdrawal of the United Kingdom from the European Exchange Rate mechanism (ERM) cost the country £3.4 billion in 24 hours. With an air of incompetence already haunting him, Major was harassed further by a revolt of several of his own MPs, who were unhappy about the negotiations then under way to expand the European Union. The Conservative Party also was embarrassed by a series of allegations about corruption, or "sleaze."

Blair's dynamic confidence contrasted sharply with Major's unhappy desperation. On May 1, 1997, the voters of the United Kingdom delivered their verdict. Labour gained a remarkable 147 MPs, the greatest victory in the party's history. The Conservatives had their worst showing in nearly a century; they won no seats at all in Scotland and Wales. For the first time in his life, Gordon Brown stepped out of the shadow cabinet to enter government office.

CHAPTER

4

The Iron Chancellor

THE DAY AFTER LABOUR'S SMASHING 1997 ELECTION VICTORY, GORDON Brown was appointed chancellor of the exchequer of Great Britain and Northern Ireland. He was to hold this position for more than 10 years, becoming in the process Labour's longest-ever serving chancellor of the exchequer. Indeed, one has to go back to Nicholas Vansittart, a contemporary of Napoleon and Thomas Jefferson, to find a politician who held the job for a longer time. Brown's accomplishment is all the more impressive when one considers that he is famous for losing his wallet and never having cash on hand. As a university undergraduate, his running of his personal expenses was so haphazard that his mother once marched him into his local bank branch to sort out his overdraft. The "Iron Chancellor," as he became known in the press, seems to be a good deal better at managing other people's money than his own.

THE CHANCELLOR

The job of chancellor of the exchequer is a very old one. The first man to hold the post in the English Parliament did so in 1316, in the reign of King Edward II. The position's name refers to the large cloth on which tokens representing money used to be placed for accounting purposes. The cloth traditionally had a pattern that resembled that of a chessboard: It was checkered, hence "exchequer."

Britain's chancellor, as he usually is known in abbreviated form, plays a role in government that is somewhat akin to that of the secretary of the treasury in the United States. The chancellor has a much more visible public profile, however. The chancellor is responsible for all government economic matters. He (so far, it has always been a he; as of this writing, no woman has held the post) decides on the scope and distribution of government spending and sets the nation's level of taxation. Historically, the chancellor also told the Bank of England at what level interest rates should be pegged. On entering office, one of Gordon Brown's first acts was to eliminate that responsibility.

The chancellor's most significant act is the preparation of the annual budget bill that lays out, in detail, the government's spending plans for the year ahead and any changes the government intends to make to taxation. The contents of the budget are kept secret until the last minute and are a source of intense speculation on the part of politicians and the media. On the day of the budget's announcement, the chancellor displays the budget box, a red case containing his speech, to the waiting press. This tradition began in the nineteenth century. For more than a hundred years, the same budget box was used by successive chancellors, until it had to be retired because it had become so battered.

Budgets are announced in March, just before the start of the new tax year, which begins in early April. At the beginning of the 1990s, however, chancellors began to make preliminary "Autumn Statements" in November. These preparatory

During the 1997 parliamentary elections, Gordon Brown *(above)* was said to work 18 hours a day. His hard work helped usher in a victorious new age for the Labour Party, which won an unprecedented 147 seats in the British Parliament. For his efforts, Brown was appointed as British chancellor of the exchequer.

speeches circulated the basic details of the upcoming budgets. It was decided to do this to tie major announcements to the beginning of the new calendar year. To some extent, this policy reduced the significance of the March budget speech. As chancellor, Gordon Brown followed this policy.

The chancellor works in the magnificent Treasury buildings along Whitehall, the avenue in central London's borough of Westminster that runs from Trafalgar Square to the Houses of Parliament and that contains most of the country's most important government offices. The chancellor's official residence is a few hundred yards away, at Number 11 Downing Street, next door to the prime minister's more famous home at Number 10. Although most of the space in the Downing Street residences is taken up with offices and conference rooms, both Number 10 and Number 11 have modestly sized apartments on top in which the prime minister's and chancellor's families live. Tony Blair was the first prime minister in recent times to bring young children with him when he arrived in Downing Street, and it quickly became clear that the apartment above Number 10 was far too small for a family of five. Blair swapped places with Brown, who at the time was single and childless and so had less need for the chancellor's larger premises.

Few jobs in British politics are as powerful as that of chancellor of the exchequer. Although in principle, he is just one member of the prime-minister's cabinet, in practice, he ranks alongside the home secretary (roughly equivalent to the United States attorney general) and the foreign secretary (Britain's secretary of state) as one of its three most senior members. Given this prominence, it is not surprising that the job often has been a springboard to further political power. Aside from Brown, eight other chancellors went on to become prime minister during the twentieth century. The job of chancellor is not an easy one, however. It is the chancellor's responsibility, as purse holder of the nation, to tax and to spend. He must demand with one hand and refuse to pay out with the other. "The chancellor," wrote one former office-holder, "is entrusted with a certain amount of misery which it is his duty to distribute as fairly as he can." This responsibility means power, but it also, at times, brings unpopularity. Additionally, the job requires a technical knowledge of finance and economics that probably has been beyond some of its less able holders. Winston Churchill's father, Lord Randolph Churchill, served briefly as chancellor during the Victorian period of the nineteenth century. The elder Churchill apparently did not understand how decimals worked: "I never could make out what those dots meant," he complained afterward.

BROWN GETS TO WORK

As Labour's new chancellor in 1997, Gordon Brown had to bear a particularly weighty burden. Every previous Labour government had experienced an economic crisis almost immediately on assuming power and had spent much of its time in office trying to fix the mess. Despite the lackluster performance of John Major's Conservative administration, Labour at the end of the 1990s was still associated in the popular mind with economic failure. It was Brown's job to alter this perception.

He decided to begin his tenure as chancellor with a public-relations coup. Three days after taking office he asked the governor of the Bank of England, Eddie George, to meet him at the Treasury. George later admitted that he thought he was going to be fired. Instead, Brown announced that he was handing over responsibility for setting interest rates to the Bank of England itself. The rate at which a central, state-owned bank such as the Bank of England charges interest helps to determine the expansion or contraction of the money supply in the economy. The rate can be lowered to encourage borrowing and growth and can be raised if there is a danger of inflation. Previously, the chancellor had made these decisions himself. This arrangement had long been criticized, however, because chancellors inevitably were tempted to meddle with the interest rate for

During Brown's chancellorship, the share of Britain's gross domestic product (GDP) paid in tax rose from 39.3 percent to 42.4 percent.

short-term political gain—to promote a spending boom right before a general election, for example—rather than to set the rate according to the best long-term interests of the economy. Brown's decision to give the governor of the Bank of England the same sort of independence enjoyed by the chairman of the United States Federal Reserve was widely welcomed, even by opponents of the Labour government. The decision helped to encourage confidence among City of London investors that the new Labour administration was serious about financial responsibility.

Brown knew that his tax policy would be under heavy scrutiny. He had not forgotten John Smith's fatal error during the 1992 election campaign. Before entering office, Brown had pledged that Labour would not increase the rate of personal income tax on either the rich or the poor. During his service as chancellor, Brown in fact reduced the rate at which most ordinary workers paid taxes, from 23 percent to 20 percent. He also cut corporate and small-business tax rates. This is not the whole story, however. Some of Brown's critics charge that he introduced "stealth taxes" while chancellor. For example, as he cut the basic tax rate, he also lowered the minimum income level at which it was necessary to pay tax at all. He also introduced some discreet technical changes to the way that taxes were levied on pension earnings that increased the overall tax burden. A recent report by an international monitoring group, the Organization for Economic Co-operation and Development, (OECD) suggests that during Brown's chancellorship, the share of Britain's gross domestic product (GDP) paid in tax rose from 39.3 percent to 42.4 percent. At this

Because he assured the public that he would not raise taxes, Gordon Brown enacted several changes that would help keep his promise and yet also benefit the British economy. *Above*, Brown *(center)* entertains advisors from his treasury department during breakfast at his residence before announcing the national budget.

point, the debate about Brown the revenue collector tends to bog down into arguments about obscure technical points and is probably irresolvable. What is clear, however, is that, rightly or wrongly, Brown successfully avoided being labeled as a heavy taxer—a first for a Labour chancellor.

Spending was the other main litmus test of his performance. Like politicians in all democratic societies today, Brown faced a dilemma: The electorate dislikes being taxed, but it also dislikes having its government services taken away. That these two positions are logically inconsistent does not help at election time. Brown announced that he would stick to the spending limits previously announced by the outgoing Conservative government; it was not until 2000 that he unveiled a major increase in expenditure for the NHS and education. Later, borrowing an idea from the American Clinton administration, Brown introduced a reform of the welfare-state system: He shifted the way benefits were distributed, from straightforward cash payments to tax credits. The idea was to create incentives for low-income citizens to earn more rather than simply to become dependent on government handouts. The results have been mixed. On the one hand, it has been estimated that Brown's reforms encouraged 50,000 single mothers, among others, to enter part-time work. The complicated rules associated with the tax credits have caused confusion, however, and have opened opportunities for widespread fraud. One of Brown's former colleagues, David Blunkett, has described the scheme as a "shambles."

CONTROVERSY

Not everyone was impressed by the Iron Chancellor, as this parody of a 1970s rock song called "Golden Brown" makes clear:

> Gordon Brown—tax me, go on!
> Take my money—almost all gone!
> With New Labour in,
> We'll just never win.
> Ever a frown, with Gordon Brown.

Brown certainly made errors, both in terms of failed policies and in terms of public relations. His opponents grumbled that in Brown's first three years as chancellor, Britain's tax code grew by 800 pages, thereby making the tax laws even more incomprehensible. Brown's decision to sell off a large proportion of the United Kingdom's gold reserves at a time when gold was trading at a historic low value was condemned as a waste of national assets. Nor were his missteps confined to economic matters alone. In 2000, Brown became enmeshed in a dispute about access to higher education for lower-income families. The controversy began because of news stories about Laura Spence, a talented student from a state-run high school in the working-class northeast of England. Spence was refused admittance to Oxford University because, it was claimed, she "did not show potential." She then went on to be admitted to Harvard University, in the United States. Brown picked up on the issue, claiming that it was an "absolute scandal" that such a prodigious student could not gain entry to one of Britain's best universities. He accused Oxford of being prejudiced toward students from historically deprived regions. Oxford officials hotly denied the charge, claiming that Brown had got his facts wrong. Spence herself said little about the quarrel. She later admitted, however, that she had not performed as well at her Oxford interview as she might have and that the university had not acted improperly in denying her a place. Brown's use of a teenager who had not asked for his help seemed, to some, crude and manipulative.

Gaffes such as this aside, however, even Brown's harshest critics have had to accept that his time as chancellor was one of consistent growth in the British economy—perhaps the only benchmark that really matters. GDP expanded by an average of 2.7 percent during Brown's chancellorship. That was higher than the European Union mean. It was an impressive feat by any account and unprecedented for a Labour government. Unemployment fell during the same period, from 7 percent to 5.5 percent, again, beating the European average. To what extent this success should be credited to Brown personally is, of course, disputed. The Conservatives have pointed out that Britain's steady economic performance began under John Major's administration, and that Brown and Blair simply reaped the benefits of years of careful Tory husbanding, both by Major and by Margaret Thatcher before him. Brown, naturally enough, rejects this interpretation. To him, Labour embraced the most beneficial aspects of the Thatcherite revolution while rejecting its harsh treatment of the poor and the disenfranchised.

LOVE AND TRAGEDY

"You've got to learn to fall in love faster and get married," Neil Kinnock advised Brown in 1990. His suggestion was as much political as personal. Historically, it has proved very difficult for a bachelor to become prime minister; during the last 100 years, only Edward Heath managed it, and he was widely criticized for what was regarded as his cold and aloof personality. Voters prefer married men and women, especially those with children. Brown kept his seemingly empty personal life so private that in August 2000, during the third year of his chancellorship, his announcement that he was to marry his girlfriend, Sarah Macaulay, astonished many people.

In fact, Brown and Macaulay dated quietly for six years before their wedding. Twelve years younger than Brown, Macauley is the daughter of a publisher and a teacher. She spent part of her childhood in the African country of Tanzania. After majoring in psychology at the University of Bristol, she went to work for a public-relations firm that did business with the Labour Party. Although she had met Brown briefly on previous occasions, their first long encounter was on an airplane trip in 1994 when they were seated next to each other. Macaulay, like Brown, was shy but assertive in her opinions. The mutual attraction was obvious. Soon, they began to see each other regularly. Fiercely protective of his privacy, however, Brown insisted on keeping the relationship out of the public eye.

The two kept up a shadowy secret life in darkened London restaurants and bars. It was not until 1997 that a British newspaper caught wind of the romance. Brown's press agent had

"I DON'T THINK WE'LL BE THE SAME AGAIN," BROWN LATER SAID, "BUT IT HAS MADE US THINK OF WHAT'S IMPORTANT. IT HAS MADE US THINK THAT YOU'VE GOT TO USE YOUR TIME PROPERLY."

—Gordon Brown

tipped off the paper in the hope that news of his relationship with Sarah would humanize the Chancellor's steely reputation. Even so, there continued to be few public sightings of the couple together until the announcement of their marriage. The quiet ceremony took place in Brown's home county of Fife. Soon after becoming Mrs. Brown (unlike Tony Blair's wife, Cherie Booth, Sarah made a point of adopting her husband's surname), the Treasury's new first lady began to introduce some order into the chancellor's chaotic home life.

Brown's newfound happiness was greater still when he revealed in July 2001 that Sarah was expecting a baby. A little girl, Jennifer, was born seven weeks prematurely on December 28, and, despite her small size, her health initially was thought to be fine. "I've probably waited longer than most people to become a father," said Brown, "and it's a superb feeling. Every father says his baby daughter is the most beautiful in the world. But she is, and we are so delighted." Within a few days, however, Jennifer suffered a brain hemorrhage. The baby was in critical condition. The Browns kept up a vigil at their daughter's side until she died, just a little more than a week after her birth. The devastated chancellor remained away from work for the next three weeks. In their daughter's memory, the couple later established the Jennifer Brown Research Fund, which provides financial aid to scientists investigating pregnancy complications, and PiggyBankKids, a charity for disadvantaged children. "I don't think we'll be the same again," Brown later said, "but it has made us think of what's important. It has made us think that you've got to use your time properly."

In October 2003, Sarah gave birth to a second child, John, and in July 2006, they had another boy, James. John has had no health problems. When James was three months old, however, the Browns revealed that he had been diagnosed with cystic fibrosis, an incurable disease of the lungs and digestive system that typically causes slow disability and premature death in adulthood. Gordon and Sarah responded stoically to the news. They thanked the public for their sympathetic messages and continue to hope that with proper treatment, James can live a normal life.

"THE QUIET LANDSLIDE"

By the time Brown married, in August 2000, the country already was gearing up for the next general election. This was the electorate's first opportunity to cast its vote on New Labour's performance while in office. Tony Blair "went to the country," as it is known, in July of the following year. The election results left very little changed. Labour lost six MPs, and the Conservatives gained one. Blair's majority from the previous election was so large, however, that this barely altered his support in the House of Commons. The campaign provoked an unusually small amount of attention and was dubbed "the quiet landslide" by the press.

On the face of it, the 2001 election results must have brought a moment or two of great satisfaction to Gordon Brown. This was the first time that a Labour government had ever won reelection with such a firm majority, and the reason was, in no small measure, due to the chancellor's successful shepherding of the economy. At last, apparently, Brown had dispelled the aura of financial incompetence that had hovered over Labour. The news was not all good, however. Overall voter turnout was the lowest since 1918: Just 59 percent of those eligible bothered to cast their ballots. This was hardly a sign

One of the few bachelors to ever take government office in Great Britain, Gordon Brown was notoriously private about his personal life. He was so successful in concealing his love life from the public, many were surprised when he wed his girlfriend of six years, Sarah Macauley. *Above*, Brown and Macaulay pose for photos after their wedding ceremony.

of widespread enthusiasm for New Labour's achievements. In fact, the reason for the party's 2001 election success lay as much in the absence of a persuasive alternative than in any positive endorsement by the British people for Blair's government.

After the catastrophe of 1997, the Conservatives had fallen into even greater disarray. They seemed to be more interested in fighting among themselves than in governing Britain. The Tories elected an intelligent but uninspiring new leader, William Hague, who failed to unite the party's warring factions in time for the 2001 election match-up with Labour. Hague quit after the defeat, and the Tory faithful elected an even more forgettable MP, Iain Duncan Smith, as party leader. Duncan Smith lasted barely two years before being turned out. Blair was lucky in his opponents.

Labour had shed its old reputation for mismanagement, but the party had gained a new one for cynicism and dishonesty. Critics on the left complained that New Labour was just Thatcherism in disguise—a flashy appeal to the public's selfishness without any genuine concern for the party's old principles of social justice and fairness. Critics on the right blasted Blair's government for its obsession with publicity and for manipulating the news with "spin." The Labour Party also was beset by scandals, mostly over money.

Peter Mandelson, the architect of Labour's original rebranding in the 1980s, had to resign in December 1998 because he had failed to reveal a loan from a rich colleague who was under investigation by Mandelson's own government department. After 10 months, Mandelson was reappointed to office but had to quit again after he was accused of interfering in the citizenship application of a well-connected Indian businessman. "Sleaze" stories such as these did much to eat away at the public confidence Labour had enjoyed in 1997. There was another problem, too. The two leaders of the party, Blair and Brown, clearly were fighting it out for dominance within the government. The chapter that follows will discuss in more detail this fascinating, decades-long, love-hate relationship.

5

Brown and Blair: A Difficult Partnership

"THAT BLAIR FELLOW—HE'S QUITE CLEVER." THIS IS THE FIRST KNOWN comment that Gordon Brown ever made about Tony Blair. He made it a few weeks after the 1983 general election, when the two new MPs were paired up in the same cramped Westminster office. Brown presumably could not have guessed how much the "clever fellow" he shared space with would go on to dominate his professional life. But, then, no one could have imagined that Blair, then just 30 years old, quite soon would go on to lead and revolutionize the Labour Party.

TONY BLAIR

Blair, like Brown, is a Scot. Born in Edinburgh in 1953, he was educated at the Scottish capital's elite school, Fettes. Unlike Brown, however, Blair always has regarded himself as culturally English. His father, Leo, was a lawyer and university lecturer.

Leo Blair was a communist in his youth, but he later turned to Conservatism. He was planning to stand for election as an MP when his aspirations for a career in public life were ended by a stroke. Initially, Tony Blair took more of an interest in rock and roll than in politics. While studying law at Oxford University, he played guitar for a band called Ugly Rumours. The band's chances at stardom were never great: They played only six gigs before disbanding, and Blair's main talent, apparently, was his knowledge of all the words to Rolling Stones songs.

It was during his time at Oxford that Blair met Cherie Booth, whom he married in 1980. After college, he enrolled as a trainee lawyer and shortly afterward joined the Labour Party. A few years later, he revived the old family ambition of a political career. He gained attention within the party in early 1982, when he made a credible, though unsuccessful, campaign for a parliamentary seat. Blair made enough of an impression to gain nomination for a much safer Labour seat in Sedgefield, in the northeast of England, in the general election the following year. This time, he won. The Blair of 1983 seems to have been a conventional socialist politician: He supported, without dissent, the party's "suicide note" left-wing manifesto.

Like his new colleague Gordon Brown, Blair soon set about making a name for himself at Westminster. A supporter of the reforming leader Neil Kinnock, he entered the shadow cabinet in 1988. His charismatic performance on camera as a Labour spokesman caught the eye of Peter Mandelson. Blair was given a prominent role in the 1992 general-election campaign that Labour narrowly lost. The period between this defeat and John Smith's death in 1994 was to prove crucial to the fortunes of both Blair and Brown. Up to this point, Brown, the slightly older man, had dominated the partnership and was seen as the more likely of the two to succeed to the leadership. Indeed, Blair, although ambitious himself, had tried to persuade his friend Brown to stand for the post of party leader in 1992, when Kinnock resigned. Either out of loyalty to Smith or because he

Charming and charismatic, Tony Blair was able to impress the leaders of the Labour Party and easily won a seat in the national parliament. Though he respected and admired Gordon Brown, their relationship changed when party officials chose Blair over Brown for a prominent government position after the 1997 elections. *Above*, Blair *(left)* and Michael Foot *(right)*, the Labour Party leader at the time Brown and Blair entered the House of Commons.

thought his chances were low, Brown drew back. Blair apparently never felt the same way about his colleague again.

When John Smith took over, he appointed Blair shadow home secretary. In many ways, this became a controversial decision. Traditional Labour supporters accused Blair of trying to be more Conservative than the Conservatives in his "tough on crime" stance. Blair clearly captured the mood of the public, however, and Peter Mandelson, the party kingmaker, became convinced that this was the man who could take Labour to victory. By summer 1993, people who once had spoken of "Brown-Blair" now referred to "Blair-Brown," a subtle but significant switch. When Smith died, it was the younger man who had the electoral edge, a fact that Blair apparently was able to exploit in the Granita deal.

CHALK AND CHEESE

Part of the fractious nature of the Blair-Brown relationship has been that they are very different kinds of men—"as different as chalk and cheese," as the British expression puts it.

Brown is an intellectual. He is a historian by training and proud of it: He used to go on vacation with suitcases packed full of books. He is a workaholic and has been known to spend up to 18 hours a day in his office after an hour of exercise on the treadmill. He speaks in sometimes incomprehensible jargon: He can say things like "post-neoclassical endogenous growth theory" with a straight face. In fact, Brown's face rarely appears to be anything other than straight. His old friend Robin Cook said that he had "a face like a wet winter's morning in Fife." This was not intended as a compliment. Colleagues insist that Brown can be charming and funny in private and among trusted friends. He finds it hard to extend this warmth beyond his close circle of allies, however. He finds the company of strangers discomforting, and he can be a clumsy conversationalist. He is, in short, the last person with whom one would

BLAIR WAS HAPPY TO GIVE INTERVIEWS ABOUT HIS CAR, HIS MUSIC COLLECTION, HIS GUITAR, EVEN HIS TASTE IN HAIRCUTS.

want to share a quiet meal or a drink. "He's an iceman," one commentator has complained.

Blair—"Call me Tony," he famously insisted—was always, by contrast, a classic smoothie. Even his bitterest opponents had to concede that he was a master in front of the camera as he delivered sound bites with eloquence and apparent sincerity. Britain's Princess Diana died in August 1997, a few months after Blair became prime minister. His televised eulogy for "the people's princess" was a work of genius that catapulted him into place as the nation's chief mourner, ahead of the royal family itself. Blair was happy to give interviews about his car, his music collection, his guitar, even his taste in haircuts. He reveled in his image as the "ordinary bloke" who could speak to the voters in the everyday language that they understood. The fact that Blair also had a young and telegenic family did not hurt, either. In 2000, Cherie Booth gave birth to the Blairs' fourth child, Leo. He was first newborn baby to live at 10 Downing Street for more than 150 years. Pictures of the proud new parents reinforced the image of Blair as a solid family man. Not everyone was convinced, of course. One critic referred to him as "a pathological confidence-trickster." If that was true, it was a con that had worked.

There were other differences, too. Unusually for a British politician, Blair made no secret of the fact that he held a strong Christian faith. He attended church services regularly and "wore his heart on his sleeve" about his belief in religious values. Although previously an Anglican, a few months after he stepped down as prime minister, Blair formally converted to Catholicism. This was something that he apparently had delayed until the end of his political career so as not to cause controversy in a traditionally Protestant country such as Great Britain.

Brown, despite being the son of a minister, has never shown a similar interest in religion. Whatever his beliefs may be, he keeps any private faith very much to himself. He is said to dislike the Presbyterian Church's emphasis on predestination—the conviction that one's behavior in life makes no difference to one's chances of eventual salvation. "The idea that it doesn't matter what you do, that you could be predetermined for damnation," as he put it, does not appeal to this strong believer in education and progress.

Despite the difference in the two men's religious outlooks, however, Blair seemed to take an oddly more materialistic interest in the world. During Blair's years as prime minister, he and Cherie had a definite taste for the high life. They often vacationed in luxurious holiday houses provided by millionaire friends. Cherie Blair got herself into some hot water for charging large fees for speeches and personal appearances and for financial dealings with a convicted Australian conman named Peter Foster. In contrast, Brown appears to be largely indifferent to property. Until his marriage, his houses were famously unfurnished. He still does not have a driver's license, and as chancellor, he chose to use a modest Ford as his ministerial vehicle rather than the usual luxury Jaguar.

Brown's advisers have tried to make him appear more human and approachable, although only with limited success. As the likelihood of his becoming prime minister drew nearer, "Project Gordon" was unveiled. It was an attempt to make Brown appear more personable to the voters. He was persuaded to replace the faded and unironed shirts he always wore with stylish new ones. He also suggested to the media that he watched reality TV, used an iPod, and liked fashionable bands such as the Arctic Monkeys. None of this came across as very convincing.

Part of Brown's problem is simply that he is very Scottish in what is overwhelmingly an English nation. Scottishness is not necessarily seen as a bad thing by the English: The Scots have a reputation for competence and efficiency—a reputation that

Brown was, of course, only too pleased to take advantage of. To English voters, however, Scots can come across as cold and aloof. There is a Scottish dialect word, *thrawn*, that means difficult, obstinate, or stubborn. Brown is very thrawn. Additionally, he came to prominence as a politician at a time when the Labour Party had not had an English leader for 11 years. Blair, although technically Scottish himself, had an advantage: He spoke with an accent similar to that of most British voters.

THE RIVALS CLASH

As soon as Labour entered office in 1997, Brown acted quickly to enforce his power within the new cabinet. He pressured Blair to give jobs to members of his own close circle—fellow MPs loyal to the chancellor who became known as "Brownites." These included Harriet Harman, who was put in charge of welfare, and Alistair Darling, who was made Brown's deputy at the Treasury. Darling later became Prime Minister Brown's own chancellor. The Brownites were lined up against the "Blairites," Labour politicians who were fiercely supportive of the prime minister. Among the Blairites were Margaret Beckett, the secretary of state for trade and industry, and David Blunkett, who was given charge of education and employment. By 1997, Peter Mandelson was definitely a Blairite. Despite his onetime support for Brown, Mandelson now was firmly a Blair man. Chancellor Brown had never forgiven Mandelson for his role in the Granita deal, a matter in which Brown now felt he had been outmaneuvered.

Perhaps the most powerful and dangerous Blairite of all, however, was Alistair Campbell. Campbell was not in the cabinet; in fact, he was not even an MP. A former journalist, he was appointed the prime minister's director of communications. This meant that Campbell was responsible for the government's publicity and relationship with the press. Blair knew very well that hostile newspaper coverage had badly damaged Labour's chances in the past. After the 1992 general election, a popular

As the youngest British prime minister in the twentieth century, Tony Blair *(right)* established an easy, casual connection with the media. Gordon Brown *(left)*, however, was perceived as dour and insisted on maintaining his privacy. Though the two politicians were able to work together successfully, their relationship was often contentious.

pro-Conservative tabloid paper called *The Sun* even boasted that it had won John Major's victory for him. There was, in fact, a grain of truth to this. Blair was determined to get the media on his side, and he placed great emphasis on establishing a good rapport with the newspapers. This was Campbell's job, and he did it very effectively, with a mixture of bribes (exclusive access to news) and threats (denial of such news).

Campbell's position as the shadowy power behind the throne—not officially a member of the government, yet probably more influential than any mere MP—was similar in kind to the position held by Karl Rove in George W. Bush's White House: a figure of respect, but also one of fear. Campbell does not seem to have been outright hostile to Gordon Brown, but his ultimate loyalty lay with the prime minister, and he was accused of using leaks and other somewhat underhanded tactics to discredit Blair's enemies.

What real differences were there between the Brownites and the Blairites? Certainly, there were some disagreements. Brown's power base was in the traditionally socialist, working-class communities of Scotland. He may have taken on board a lot of New Labour ideas, but he still was, fundamentally, a believer in a strong welfare state and direct government responsibility for fixing social problems. These were the sort of "Old Labour" policies that the Blairites now shunned. Brown's supporters felt that the prime minister had become so Thatcherite that he was now indistinguishable from the Conservatives that he supposedly opposed. The Brownites could not come out openly and say this, of course, but in their speeches and statements, there were subtle suggestions of unhappiness. In 2003, Brown himself is believed to have hinted at this in his major speech to the Labour Party's annual conference. Labour, he said, "needed not just a program but a soul"; the party was "best when it was boldest, best when it was united, best when it was Labour."

There also was the issue of Europe. Ever since Britain joined the European Economic Community—now called the European Union—in 1973, the "European question" has divided the country's politicians. Broadly speaking, they are divided into "Europhiles" and "Europhobes": those who want greater involvement in the EU and those who want to keep their distance from it. This difference of opinion transcends the traditional party divide. There are Europhile Tories and Europhobe Tories, with Labour equally split.

The Conservatives had fallen apart during the 1990s in nasty public quarrels about Europe; Blair's government was careful to avoid any obvious division on the subject. It became clear, however, that the prime minister was much more of a Europhile than Chancellor Brown. In 1997, the most immediate aspect of the European question that faced Blair's government was whether the United Kingdom should take part in the planned single European currency scheme and replace the pound with the new euro. Arguments about whether adapting the euro was in Britain's best financial interest rolled on throughout the summer. In October, Chancellor Brown announced that the United Kingdom would adopt the euro, but only if five economic tests (for example, would adapting the euro help the British economy to grow?) all were met.

Crucially, the Treasury would decide whether these tests were met. This meant that Brown, not the prime minister, ultimately would decide when Britain would enter the "Eurozone." Throughout his time as chancellor, Brown declared that the five tests still had not been met. Because Brown seems so lukewarm about Britain's adopting the euro, some onlookers believe that the five tests were designed to be impossible to meet, thereby putting the question off permanently.

It is possible, however, that too much emphasis has been placed on the gulf in policy between the Brownites and the Blairites. One Scottish journalist has argued that the distinction between the two "is more tribal than ideological"; in other words, the two sides differ more over personal ambition, distrust, and old grudges than they do over substantive differences of opinion.

"ANYONE BUT GORDON"

Because the two men had to maintain a public show of unity, the Blair-Brown squabble was conducted by proxy. "Unnamed spokespersons" often leaked information to the press. Blair's aides complained that the chancellor was "empire-building" in Whitehall, seizing control of policies, such as education and health, that he had no right to meddle in. Brown, they claimed, was a disruptive, almost childish presence in the cabinet, like "a mad relative in the attic, constantly banging the floor with a saucepan." Suggestions that Brown was consumed by pride and jealousy were fed to the papers. "Gordon is extraordinarily, unbelievably arrogant," the Blairites wrote, "a man consumed by bitterness." The most serious accusation in this campaign was made in 2000, allegedly by Alistair Campbell himself, when a news story alleged that the chancellor was "psychologically flawed" and too unstable ever to be trusted as prime minister.

In September 2004, as Labour geared up for its second reelection campaign, Blair suggested on television that if he were elected prime minister again, he would serve out a full term before leaving Downing Street for good. This would mean that by the end of that new term, he would have been prime minister for 13 years, thus breaking the terms of the Granita pact. Brown could say nothing in public. Secretly, however, he is supposed to have been outraged. "There is nothing that you could say to me now that I could ever believe," he is alleged to have told Blair. For his part, the prime minister is whispered to have thought of sacking his chancellor if the election results were impressive enough, thereby getting rid of the Brownite problem in one fell swoop. Whether or not these rumors are

Even once-loyal Blairites were starting to grumble that the prime minister had been around too long and was becoming a liability.

true may be known one day; for now, no one is admitting anything.

The election was held in May 2005. Labour won again, although with a considerably reduced majority of MPs. Blair now had an advantage over the other parties of only 66 seats. The fact that Blair won at all should not be underestimated, however, especially as the controversy over the Iraq war was then at its height. The victory was a testimony not only to the political effectiveness of Blair and Brown, but also to the "spin" skills of Alistair Campbell. Voter turnout was almost as low as in 2001, however, and Labour probably still owed much of its success to the weakness of the Conservative Party rather than to voter confidence in Labour's own achievements. The electorate had given Blair a half-hearted mandate to continue. Perhaps most dangerous of all, the Tories picked a new leader, David Cameron. Cameron was 13 years younger than Blair. He also was energetic, media friendly, and an appealing "compassionate conservative." All of these were the sorts of charismatic traits that the prime minister once had been praised for. The chance of Labour's winning again in 2010 was beginning to look a bit bleak.

With his Labour government in this fragile state, any chance that Blair had once had to remove Brown had disappeared. Instead, it was Blair's own head that now was on the chopping block. Even once-loyal Blairites were starting to grumble that the prime minister had been around too long and was becoming a liability. Surely, it would be better to give a new leader time to prove himself before the next election. Blair promised that there would be a "smooth and

When the Labour Party won the 2005 election, Tony Blair declared that he would serve a full third term, which violated his "Granita Deal" with Brown. When he showed no signs of leaving office, a group of Labour MPs demanded Blair's resignation. Blair had no choice but to comply. *Above*, Blair blows a kiss into the crowd after announcing his resignation.

orderly transition," but he refused to give concrete details. On September 5, 2006, 17 Labour MPs publicly demanded that the prime minister resign. Two days later, Blair announced that he would step down sometime before September 2007.

The king was, if not dead, on his deathbed. Who would seize the crown? Brown was the obvious candidate, but furious rumors began that loyal Blairites were waging a behind-the-scenes "ABG" campaign: "Anyone but Gordon." The names of a number of possible rivals to Brown were floated. One name mentioned was that of David Miliband, an up-and-coming young member of the cabinet who, it was argued, would be a more effective rival to David Cameron than the aging and sulky chancellor. The ABG campaign never developed enough critical mass to succeed, however. When Blair resigned as party leader in May 2007, the only opposition Brown had for the Labour leadership post was from a diehard "Old Labour" candidate, a man who failed to get enough nominations even to get on the ballot.

Blair gave lip service to the idea that he supported Brown. Just before the election, he praised his old colleague as "an extraordinary and rare talent . . . as someone who has known him for over 20 years as a friend and a colleague, he can make a real difference to this country for the better and for the good. I wish him well and, as I say, I'm delighted to support him and endorse him fully." Critics noted that this endorsement came very late in the day. Still, it was enough. On June 27, Blair went to the queen to tender his resignation as prime minister. The same day, Brown was summoned to Buckingham Palace to "kiss hands," as it is known, with the monarch. His day had come at last.

CHAPTER

6

Brown's Vision for Britain

IN 2007, IN ADDITION TO BECOMING PRIME MINISTER, GORDON BROWN published two books. One, *Britain's Everyday Heroes*, was a portrayal of 33 ordinary members of the public who had performed exceptional feats of community spirit. It was a well-meant tribute to deserving people, but it was not a book that Brown seems to have had much personal involvement in writing. The other book, however, appears to have come much more from Brown's heart. *Courage: Eight Portraits* contains mini-biographies of people such as Martin Luther King, Jr., Nelson Mandela, the Nazi resister Dietrich Bonhoeffer, and Cicely Saunders, the founder of the British hospice movement for terminally ill people. Brown evidently has admired many of these people since childhood, and he writes about them with sincerity and admiration.

The most interesting portrait in the book is probably that of Robert F. Kennedy, brother of the assassinated American

In 2007, when Gordon Brown accepted the position of British prime minister, he also became a published author. One of his books, *Courage: Eight Portraits* included a profile of Robert F. Kennedy *(above)*, a U.S. politician and brother of President John F. Kennedy. Just as the Kennedy brothers had been embroiled in the Vietnam War controversy, the new prime minister had to find a way to reduce Britain's unpopular military commitment in Iraq.

president John F. Kennedy. Robert Kennedy was also a politician; he was slain by a gunman during his primary bid for the presidency in 1968. Robert Kennedy, Brown writes, was a man "caught between his deeply felt moral and strategic qualms and his shrewd understanding" that those passions had to be translated into realistic political action. Brown also notes that despite Kennedy's compassion for America's poor, "his starting point for empowerment was that work, not benefits, offered the way out of poverty . . . he came to the view that too much welfare left the poor dependent." It was intellectual courage such as this, Brown argues, the ability "to embed the demand for justice in practical politics," that was Kennedy's finest achievement. Robert Kennedy, in other words, was very much a New Labour man. The reader, perhaps, is expected to conclude that Gordon Brown is very much like Robert Kennedy. Does the new prime minister subscribe to Kennedy's view that "only those who dare to fail greatly, can ever achieve greatly"? And what would Brown like to achieve? What, in other words, is Brown's vision for Britain?

BRITAIN AFTER THATCHER

"We are all Thatcher's children now." This is a common refrain in modern Britain. In a generational sense, it is becoming increasingly true: No one under the age of 40 has any adult memory of the time before Margaret Thatcher's years as prime minister. It is also true in the sense of a shift in ideas and attitudes across all age groups. Before 1979, most Britons took for granted the existence of nationalized, state-owned industries, powerful trade unions, and an ever-growing welfare state. By the time Thatcher left office, these assumptions had become obsolete. If any Labour supporters had a lingering belief that New Labour would try to turn back the clock, they soon were sorely disappointed. Blair even was willing to say a few good words about the former prime minister, something unheard of among Labour politicians before him. "I believe Mrs. Thatcher's emphasis on enterprise was right," Blair once said. For her part, Thatcher was reported to have preferred Blair to John Major—her own successor—in the 1997 election. In the past, Gordon Brown often had spoken bitterly of the former prime minister. Within a few months of taking over at 10 Downing Street, however, he invited Thatcher to tea and had himself photographed with her. His spokespersons said that this was just a standard courtesy to an ex-PM. Others suspected that Brown was trying to curry favor with Thatcherites.

By 2002, according to the British Social Attitudes Survey, the number of people who believed that the government should help redistribute wealth from the rich to the poor had fallen to a record low. Ordinary Britons also were far less supportive of higher unemployment benefits than they had been before Thatcher. These declines were largest among Labour voters. On the other hand, the number of Britons who thought that the gap between rich and poor had grown too large had risen. Figures such as these suggested that many of the old solutions to Britain's social problems had become discredited in the public eye. From that point of view, Old Labour had been consigned permanently to the waste dump. That did not mean that most ordinary voters were happy with the shape of society, however. Clearly, the mantra that "greed is good" had not taken hold. The National Health Service, for all the dissatisfaction with its performance, remained highly popular. Britons, it seems, did not want an end to public services. They just wanted them to be run better.

Brown appears to share this view. For all of his New Labour credentials, he never has abandoned the belief that government intervention is necessary to tackle social ills such as poverty and homelessness. In the first few weeks of his time as prime minister, he announced that housing would be his government's major priority. He promised to build 3 million homes by 2020. In a very post-Thatcherite manner, however, these homes would be built with private as well as public money. Brown is particularly proud of the work he has done to relieve child poverty. Brown claims that under his chancellorship, 600,000 children were taken out of poverty. His stated goal is to halve the remaining number of children in poverty by 2010 and to eliminate child poverty altogether by 2020. His critics dispute his record, but Brown appears to take the subject very seriously. He refers to it often. "Every child should have the best start in life, everybody should have the chance of a job, nobody should be brought up suffering in poverty," he has said. "I would call those the beliefs that you associate with civilization and dignity."

Any reversal of the Tories' privatizations appears to be out. The Blair government not only declined to renationalize the old state-owned companies when it entered power, but it also continued the process. The Labour government encouraged private sector investment in the NHS and ended the Royal Mail's monopoly on postal delivery. Not all of these moves have been without controversy. In 2003, London Underground, the company that operates the capital's famous "tube" system, was semiprivatized when its day-to-day operations were handed over to two private companies. At the time, this was hailed by Labour as a breakthrough in public transportation that would eliminate problems with late trains and bad service. Instead, critics have complained that the tube has gotten worse, not better. By summer 2007, Metronet, one of the private companies, was on the brink of bankruptcy, and the Treasury was blamed for a bill of over £455 million in legal fees related to the privatization scheme. Still, state-owned businesses that are said to be earmarked for possible sale by Brown's government include the Meteorological Office, parts of the BBC, and the company that manages college loans.

A MOVE FROM "PRESIDENTIAL" POLITICS

One of the complaints about Tony Blair's style of government was that it had become increasingly "presidential." This meant that the prime minister had started to act like a U.S.-style president rather than a British prime minister. In Britain, under what is called the Westminster system, the prime minister is a powerful politician, but he is supposed to govern as the head of a committee rather than as a lone ruler making all his own decisions. He is *primus inter pares*, or "first amongst equals," as the Latin saying goes. The cabinet, the group of senior government ministers, is meant to debate and agree upon all policies before those policies are announced. Responsibility for different aspects of government such as finance, education, and foreign policy is delegated to departmental ministers who traditionally have had some independence from the prime minister. Moreover, the government as a whole has to answer to the rest of the House of Commons and must seek approval for its actions from other MPs. Parliament has the power to bring down the government any time it chooses simply by passing a "motion of no-confidence" in the government's performance. This is unlike the United States, where a sitting president can be removed from office only by the much more difficult route of an impeachment.

Blair was accused of undermining these traditions. He preferred to handle many policy decisions personally, bypassing his own cabinet ministers. The most important members of his circle often were not MPs at all, but media advisers such as Alistair Campbell. There was, it was said, no healthy sense of debate and no tolerance of disagreement within the cabinet. Ministers were there simply to rubber stamp decisions made by the prime minister, the only exception to this rule being Gordon Brown. When the defense secretary, Les Browne, took issue with Blair in one of his first cabinet meetings in 2006, there is supposed to have been shock and bewilderment around the table. This simply was not how things were done in a New Labour government. Because he had such a large majority of supporters in Parliament during his first two terms in office, Blair was accused of treating the House of Commons with

Brown has suggested, for example, that Parliament, and not the prime minister, should decide when the country goes to war

complacency and contempt. It was noted that he rarely bothered to show up and vote in debates himself. According to his critics, Blair treated Parliament as a tiresome distraction from the "real" business of government.

Whether or not these accusations were fair, when Gordon Brown took over as prime minister, he made a point of distancing himself from this sort of behavior. The former chancellor apparently has stressed that he wants to make decisions within the cabinet in a more collegial way. He also has banished media spokesmen and other spin doctors to the margins. One of his planned reforms is a review of the powers of the House of Commons. Brown has suggested, for example, that Parliament, and not the prime minister, should decide when the country goes to war—a very sensitive point, given the controversy over the invasion of Iraq.

It can be argued, of course, that Gordon Brown can be gentler with his cabinet because he does not have to deal with Gordon Brown. Blair always had his powerful chancellor at his side, threatening to stir up trouble whenever the two disagreed. To use the colorful description that began during Thatcher's administration, without a "big beast" opposing him across the table, Brown may have the luxury of appearing more open minded and willing to listen to contrary views. It also has been pointed out that for all his newfound passion for parliamentary accountability, Brown did not choose to call a general election when he became prime minister, perhaps because he was afraid that he might lose. There was no constitutional reason why he had to do so; Labour has the legal right to stay in office until 2010, no matter who its leader is. Nonetheless, it is a little uncomfortable for Labour that the most powerful man

Unlike his predecessor, Gordon Brown wanted to reestablish the style of collaborative governing that had traditionally been followed by the British prime minister. Instead of making all the decisions alone or from the advice of private advisors, Brown frequently consults with his cabinet ministers and has broadened the powers of the House of Commons, resulting in more dialogue and debate. *Above*, Brown in his first cabinet meeting as prime minister.

in Britain won his place, not by a vote of the masses, but by the support of small number of MPs.

SCOTLAND AND DEVOLUTION

The relationship between Scotland and England within the United Kingdom of Great Britain is a complicated one. Partly, this is because one has so many more people than the other: England's population is about 50 million people; Scotland's is only 5 million. The British capital, London, is in England, and until 1999 all Scottish affairs were handled at Westminster. Scotland was an independent country only 300 years ago, however, and it retains its own unique legal, educational, and religious laws. The Scots still have a lively sense of their own distinct identity, and they dislike the assumption, common amongst people outside the UK, that "Britain" is synonymous with "England."

During the 1970s, there was a movement among the Scots to regain greater autonomy for themselves, a process called *devolution*. This led to a referendum in 1978 to decide whether Scotland should have its own regional parliament again. Because of lack of enthusiasm, the vote narrowly failed. Perhaps if Margaret Thatcher had not won office the following year, the issue might have gone away. During the 17 years of Conservative administration that followed, however, it became increasingly obvious that the government in London was ruling Scotland despite having barely any following there at all. In the 1992 general election, only one in four Scottish voters supported the Tories, and only 11 of Scotland's 79 parliamentary seats went Conservative. Because of his power base in southern England, Conservative John Major got elected anyway. To many Scots, this began to seem like an intolerable position, and calls for devolution became stronger. When Labour took over in 1997, the new government passed a bill that gave Scotland a regional parliament for the first time since 1707. London remains the center of power in the United Kingdom, but the Scots now control their own policies on matters such as health, environmental law, and law and order.

Unsurprisingly, as a Scot, Brown was very supportive of the devolution movement and was the driving force behind New Labour's plans for a Scottish parliament. "It's Gordon's passion," Blair apparently said. Now that the Scottish parliament is a reality, however, the question has shifted to more radical ground. Should Scotland become completely independent from the United Kingdom? Such a move would have far greater implications for the rest of Britain than devolution ever did. If the Scottish people became citizens of their own country, what rights would they have in England? What would happen to the armed forces? And what would happen to Queen Elizabeth's role as head of state? No one really knows what would happen if the United Kingdom were to split apart. What is known is that an increasing number of Scots appear to back the idea. In 2006, according to one opinion poll, a narrow majority of Scots (52 percent) approved of a secession plan for the first time. The Scottish Nationalist Party (SNP), a movement that favors independence, has become a powerful force in the region's politics. It is now the largest party in the Scottish parliament, and it leads the government there, with Labour opposing it.

Although no one can accuse Brown of being anything other than a passionately patriotic Scot, he has emerged as one of the biggest opponents of independence. He argues that the independence movement is based more on sentimentality than on common sense. Scotland, Brown claims, would lose wealth and influence if it were divided from the rest of the UK. The SNP are an "opportunist group of nationalists playing fast-and-loose" with dangerous fantasies, he said. "It is now time for supporters of the union to speak up, to resist any drift towards a Balkanization of Britain and to acknowledge Great Britain for the success it has been and is," says Brown. Brown even makes a point of supporting the English soccer team when they play in international competitions, something that might horrify many other Scots. (Fortunately for Brown, England's team has done so badly in recent years that this hardly has been an issue.). The fact that one of their countrymen is now in power in London may have helped to dampen some of the frustration that encouraged Scottish voters to support independence during the 1990s. If the SNP continues to expand, however, Brown's position as the most visible pro-unionist in Scotland may cost him popularity.

BRITISHNESS

The question of British identity goes beyond the England-Scotland divide. The United Kingdom is now a multicultural, multiracial state. In 2001, about 8 percent of the population was nonwhite. Most of this minority population had its roots in the so-called "New Commonwealth" nations of India, Pakistan, and Jamaica. This percentage is not large, but Britain's ethnic minorities are scattered disproportionately across the country. Towns such as Leeds and Bradford have very large communities of South Asian residents, for example. This multicultural variety is also reflected in religious belief. With 1.6 million practicing Muslims in Britain, Islam is now the second-largest faith in the United Kingdom. This rapid transition, after centuries of relatively little ethnic or religious diversity, has not come without incident or concern.

The terrorist suicide bombings on July 7, 2005 (or "7/7," as it has come to be known), marked the deadliest day in London since World War II. The bombings also were al-Qaeda's most devastating blow in its war against the Western democratic nations since the Madrid train bombings a year before. What made the 7/7 attacks particularly frightening was that they were carried out by four men who had been born in Britain or (in one case) had come to live there at a very early age. These were home-grown Britons who nonetheless felt so alienated from their mother country that they were driven to kill themselves and their fellow citizens in the cause of religious war.

Was this a symptom of years of prejudice and discrimination against South Asians and other minority citizens, or was it, rather, a sign that some British residents refused to accept the country's principles of democracy and freedom and preferred, instead, to become "enemies within"? The disagreement about the moral of 7/7 has dominated public debate since the bombings. It even has emerged in trivial ways. In early 2007, British newspapers were full of stories about the reality TV show *Celebrity Big Brother*. One of the contestants, the Bollywood movie star Shilpa Shetty, accused some of the other residents in the Big Brother house of racist comments. Gordon Brown himself weighed in on the dispute during a visit to India. "There is

A terrifying bombing in the center of London in 2005 shocked and scared many throughout Great Britain. This attack, along with the Madrid train bombings in 2004, forced many European governments to carefully examine issues of diversity in their own countries. *Above*, the remains of the bus bombed in the 7/7 attacks.

> # "WE HAVE TO BE CLEARER NOW ABOUT HOW DIVERSE CULTURES WHICH INEVITABLY CONTAIN DIFFERENCES CAN FIND THE ESSENTIAL COMMON PURPOSE ALSO WITHOUT WHICH NO SOCIETY CAN FLOURISH."
>
> —Gordon Brown

a lot of support for Shilpa" back in Britain, he claimed. This showed that the United Kingdom wanted to be, in Brown's words, "defined by being a tolerant, fair and decent country."

Brown has gone on to say much about "Britishness." He has proposed the establishment of an annual "British Day" to celebrate national identity. It would take place on June 27, the day that the Victoria Cross, Britain's highest award for military gallantry, was first awarded. He also has suggested that people fly the Union Jack—the British flag— and display other visible symbols of the nation. "We have to face uncomfortable facts," Brown has said, "that while the British response to July 7 was remarkable, they were British citizens who were prepared to maim and kill fellow British citizens . . . we have to be clearer now about how diverse cultures which inevitably contain differences can find the essential common purpose also without which no society can flourish."

Opinion has been divided about this appeal to Britishness. Some Brown supporters argue that to discourage the appeal of extremism, there must be more public appreciation of British qualities and virtues. Others have suggested that such symbols are shallow and will do nothing to cement real community ties. Would 7/7 have been averted by a few more Union Jacks?

However one looks at it, the debate about Britishness and the place of ethnic diversity in the United Kingdom has been transformed by the global war on terror. The next chapter offers a look at Gordon Brown's approach to the challenge of al-Qaeda and the situation in the Middle East.

7

Brown and the Global War on Terror

ON SATURDAY AFTERNOON, JUNE 30, 2007, LESS THAN 36 HOURS AFTER Gordon Brown's appointment as prime minister, a dark green Jeep Cherokee drove into the security posts in front of the entrance to the terminal at Glasgow International Airport, Scotland's busiest, and burst into flames. Two men jumped out of the burning car, one of them on fire from head to foot. They began scuffling with police and bystanders. After the two were apprehended, it was discovered that their Jeep was packed with gasoline cans and propane canisters. Evidently, the attackers had intended to cause an even more violent explosion. The burned man was rushed to a hospital for emergency care but died from his injuries a month later. The other attacker was taken into custody. The police revealed that the alleged terrorists were both doctors. One was Indian; the other was Iraqi. Both had been recruited a year earlier to work in the United

Kingdom for the National Health Service. They were, it was quickly announced, suspected of being members of Osama bin Laden's al-Qaeda terrorist network. The police soon arrested four more men and one woman. All were foreign-born doctors or medical students believed to be connected to the attack, although three later were released without being charged.

Although the terrorists were inept, the damage they caused was slight, and service at the Glasgow airport was interrupted for only a day, the symbolism of the attack was significant. On June 29, in a possibly connected incident, two car bombs had been discovered in central London and defused before they could detonate. Although there is no hard evidence that the timing of the attempted bombings was connected to Brown's promotion to prime minister, it did seem to be oddly coincidental. The fact that one of the attacks took place in Brown's native country, which had never experienced a direct terrorist attack before (the 1988 Lockerbie jumbo-jet bombing happened by chance over western Scotland) seemed to reinforce the suspicion that there was, indeed, a link. Was Brown being tested or taunted by al-Qaeda? Did the terrorists want to rattle his new government or see what its response would be?

Brown soon chaired a meeting of Cabinet Office Briefing Room (A) (COBRA), the intelligence coordinating committee of the British government that meets to discuss serious emergencies or security threats to the nation. The "UK Threat Level," a hazard scale similar to the Homeland Security Advisory System in the United States, was briefly raised to its highest level, "critical." Later, Brown appeared on television to praise the emergency services for their rapid response and to assure the country that despite the "long-term and sustained" nature of the threat from terrorism, the country would not be cowed. "We will not yield, we will not be intimidated and we will not allow anyone to undermine our British way of life," he said.

Gordon Brown inherited the leadership of a country in which terrorism was very much on every citizen's mind. He also inherited a Labour government that had been widely criticized during the past four years for the way it had responded to the terrorist threat, both in terms of its foreign policy and also because of the implication its security measures had for civil liberties. Tony Blair's decision to take part in the invasion and postwar occupation of Iraq in 2003 had proved unpopular with voters. Some people argued that Blair's decision had increased Britain's vulnerability to attack from al-Qaeda. Measures such as the 2006 Terrorism Act, which gave the police new powers to act against suspected attackers, had proved highly divisive because of the act's potential for curtailing individual rights. One of the key votes taken during the passage of the act through Parliament had been Blair's most serious defeat in the House of Commons since he became prime minister. As chancellor, Brown had not taken a very visible role in these matters. It had long been suspected, however, that he and Blair had important differences of opinion over such matters as Iraq, terrorism, and Britain's relationship with the United States. It remains to be seen how Prime Minister Brown will maintain or change his predecessor's controversial approach to transatlantic affairs and the global war on terror.

TERRORISM IN BRITAIN

Britain's experience with terrorism did not begin with al-Qaeda. In fact, for over 30 years before 9/11, the United Kingdom had been subject to thousands of terror incidents connected to the Troubles between the Protestant majority and Catholic minority communities in Northern Ireland. Most of these incidents took place in Northern Ireland itself. It has been estimated that between 1968 and 1992, there were at least 10,000 explosions in Northern Ireland caused by paramilitary forces on either side of the conflict. There also were many more shootings, stabbings, and assaults committed by one or other faction. The Irish terrorists, particularly those who were members of the Irish Republican Army (IRA) and its various

These decades of strife meant that the British police and intelligence services had plenty of experience dealing with domestic terrorism.

splinter groups, had not restricted their activities to Northern Ireland, however. During the 1970s, 42 people were killed on the British mainland in terrorist acts connected to the Troubles. Another 33 were killed in the decade that followed. In 1984, the IRA came very close to killing Prime Minister Margaret Thatcher when they bombed the hotel she was staying in during the annual Conservative Party conference. In a particularly audacious attack in 1991, the IRA fired mortar shells into the cabinet rooms in Downing Street.

The cost in human lives brought by these attacks naturally attracted the bulk of attention, but some of the attacks had serious financial implications, too. The IRA planted a pair of huge bombs in London's financial district in 1992 and 1993. The bombs caused more than £1,800 million (about $2.5 billion) in combined damage, and the subsequent cost in compensation payouts almost brought down the famous insurance company Lloyds of London. Nor was Irish terrorism the only threat to the nation. During the 1970s, the Palestinian "Black September" terrorist group operated in Britain against Israeli targets. In that same decade, animal-rights extremists frequently sent letter bombs and other incendiary devices to scientists who did research that involved vivisection—that is, operated on live animals for investigative rather than medical reasons.

These decades of strife meant that the British police and intelligence services had plenty of experience dealing with domestic terrorism. Their level of expertise was matched, perhaps, only by that of the Israeli security forces. The British police had developed a sophisticated response to such acts. Special Branch is the plainclothes arm of the British police

Only a few hours after Gordon Brown had officially taken over as British prime minister, there was an attempted bombing of the Glasgow airport in Scotland *(above)*. A group believed to be linked to the terrorist organization al-Qaeda is suspected of planning and orchestrating the event. This incident was the latest in a series of attacks on British soil, including the 2005 bombings on London buses and subways.

force dedicated to dealing with terrorism. For many years, that branch had worked with the armed forces and the country's counterintelligence agency, MI5, to investigate and undermine the IRA and other terrorist groups such as the Protestant Ulster Volunteer Force (UVF). By a successful strategy of planting informers in terrorist cells or persuading terrorist-group members to testify in court against their colleagues—the so-called "supergrass" system—the British steadily chipped away at the Irish terrorist networks.

It is widely believed that this slow wearing away was what convinced the IRA to abandon its campaign of violence, first in 1994 and then, after a short relapse, in 1997. The IRA agreed, instead, to take part in what became known as the Northern Irish Peace Process. Throughout the years of the Troubles, the British public had become used to such security measures as closed-circuit television (CCTV) cameras in urban areas and checks of hand luggage and personal belongings when entering public buildings. Indeed, Britain has one of the most extensive surveillance networks in the world. There are believed to be more than 15 million CCTV cameras across the country—one camera for every five people.

On the one hand, then, Britain was well prepared for the Islamist terrorist threat that emerged so spectacularly on September 11, 2001. It could also be argued, however, that the Irish experience was misleading. The IRA always had been motivated by a definite, practical goal: the reunion of Northern Ireland with the Republic of Ireland. The British government's strategy was to persuade Irish nationalists that they could not achieve this by military means, only by peaceful, political ones. It is not at all clear that bin Laden's followers are interested in coming to any sort of negotiated compromise with the West short of all-out victory for one side or the other. Additionally, it may not be as easy to motivate men who are inspired to action by a religious cause and are willing—indeed, sometimes eager—to sacrifice their lives for that cause to inform on their colleagues or switch sides simply through offers of money or criminal immunity. The intelligence services are handicapped by a shortage of Arabic-speaking Muslims who might act as spies or informers. The effect of this has been a failure to preempt al-Qaeda terrorist attacks on British soil. Neither Special Branch nor MI5 were able to predict or prevent the coordinated suicide assault by al-Qaeda on London's public transport system on July 7, 2005. That attack killed 52 commuters, injured 700, and brought the British capital to a standstill for over a day.

AFGHANISTAN AND IRAQ

In October 2001, one month after 9/11, Tony Blair's government announced that it would contribute British forces to the American-led invasion of Afghanistan. This invasion was intended to remove the fundamentalist Taliban regime, a regime that had tolerated and probably encouraged the existence of al-Qaeda training camps within Afghan territory. Since the end of 2001, a considerable British military presence has existed in Afghanistan, particularly in the country's mountainous southern province of Helmand, where Taliban fighters continue to operate. Although the ongoing war against the Taliban has been long, and there is as yet no sign of any definite end, this has been, from the outset, a relatively popular conflict in Britain. About two-thirds of the electorate supported the original decision to intervene. Gordon Brown has inherited a difficult war in Afghanistan, but its political consequences at home have not been severe.

The same cannot be said about the invasion of Iraq in March 2003. About 45,000 British troops, the largest contingent aside from that of the United States, initially took part in that invasion. There is no need here to go over at length the story of how President George W. Bush decided to overthrow Saddam Hussein's regime or to describe the events that have taken place in that country since the invasion. What is important to this present story is the political effects of the Iraq War in Britain. Iraq came to dominate Tony Blair's second term in office. The war overshadowed his government's other efforts in matters such as health and education. Indeed, Blair probably will come to be defined by posterity as the man who, rightly or wrongly, gave President Bush the crucial international support to begin the conflict.

Critics in Britain did not simply charge that the United States and Great Britain had gone to war under false pretences and allege that the occupation of Iraq was a failure. They also contended that the UK's conspicuous role in support of the United States had made Britain a greater target for terrorism. This accusation gained strength when tape recordings of the 7/7 bombers were released. In those tapes, the bombers said that they were motivated by the situation in Iraq. Disputes about the war flared up throughout the last years of Blair's term.

The most serious controversy was the story of the so-called "September Dossier." The dossier was an official intelligence briefing issued to the press in late 2002. It strongly—and wrongly—suggested that Iraq possessed weapons of mass destruction (WMD), at that time the principal justification for the war. Shortly after the invasion, a series of BBC reports claimed that Blair's administration had deliberately exaggerated the evidence of Iraqi WMD in order to drum up support for the attack. One of the government's senior experts on WMD, Dr. David Kelly, had read and criticized the dossier before its publication. He later leaked his concerns to reporters. Kelly's name was made public, however, and in his distress, he committed suicide. A judicial inquiry into the affair eventually cleared Blair of any blame, but the inquiry was widely condemned by the media as a "whitewash." The prime minister's reputation plummeted. The man who in 1997 had been more popular than Winston Churchill was, by May 2006, the most disliked Labour prime minister since World War II. "Bambi," the wide-eyed idealist, had become "Phony Tony," or, more bluntly, "Bliar."

During all of this, Gordon Brown remained conspicuously silent. Rumors were widespread. Some said that the chancellor had never been very enthusiastic about the idea of invading Iraq in the first place. Other said that because the government's

WHEN HE BECAME PRIME MINISTER, BROWN MADE IT CLEAR THAT BRITAIN'S TIME IN IRAQ WAS COMING TO A CLOSE.

Iraq policy had proved so unpopular, Brown wanted to distance himself from Blair and avoid being damaged by the fallout. Brown was persuaded to make occasional murmurs of support: In September 2005, in a speech to the Labour Party conference, he said that Britain would "spend what it takes" to see victory in Iraq. Furthermore, Brown chose not to take advantage of the situation when Blair was at his weakest, such as in March 2003, when Robin Cook, Brown's old coauthor and the former foreign secretary, resigned from the cabinet in protest at the invasion. Had Brown also resigned at that point, it is quite possible that Blair himself would have been forced out. The chancellor's decision to stay loyal may have been a decision made through principle, or it may have been a simple miscalculation. Either way, Brown did not exploit Iraq as much as he might have done.

When he became prime minister, Brown made it clear that Britain's time in Iraq was coming to a close. By the beginning of 2007, the British military presence already had fallen to about 7,000 troops, most of them located in the southern city of Basra. On becoming PM, Brown announced that this drawdown in British personnel would continue throughout the year. In September, the British pulled out of Basra itself and moved to the city's airport. Three months later, they formally handed over control of the province to the Iraqi authorities. By spring 2008, only about 2,500 British soldiers were expected to remain in Iraq. Brown has argued that this reduction in manpower is because of the increase in stability in Basra. His critics suggest, however, that the drawdown has more to do with his desire to get out of a deteriorating and unpopular war.

SECURITY AND LIBERTY

Quite aside from his controversial decisions about Iraq, Blair also was accused of being heavy handed in his approach to civil liberties and of using the war on terror as an excuse to introduce new and disturbing constraints on personal freedom. The prime minister already had a reputation for alleged authoritarianism. In 1998, the Blair government introduced what it called "Anti-Social Behaviour Orders," or ASBOs, that can be applied by a court to an individual who is deemed to be a public nuisance. Such a person can be prosecuted and sent to prison for up to five years if he or she continues to act in an antisocial way.

Opinion about ASBOs is divided. Many people have argued that these orders are a necessary protection for the community: They punish acts of theft, vandalism, and harassment. Others have suggested that ASBOs lead to excessive punishments for trivial acts or even criminalize what should be legal behavior. In one case, an 87-year-old man was given an ASBO and told that he would be jailed if he made sarcastic remarks to his neighbors. Some critics alleged that Blair's attraction to ASBOs as a solution to crime demonstrated that he was a "control freak" who was unconcerned about freedom. According to one commentator, the prime minister "tended to be dismissive of people who cared about civil liberties." Blair, the commentator said, felt that "freedoms had to be sacrificed to preserve freedom. Those who did not see that were simply not living in the real world that he had to deal with."

The debate about the 2006 Terrorism Act had similarities to the ongoing dispute in the United States about the 2001 USA Patriot Act. The British act was the sixth in a series of increasingly stringent anti-terrorism laws passed since 9/11. In its original form, the 2006 Terrorism Act would have allowed police to hold terrorist suspects without charge for up to 90 days. This, Blair argued, was necessary so give the authorities time to prepare a case against alleged suicide bombers. The idea

One of Tony Blair's most unpopular decisions as prime minister was to get involved in the war in Iraq. As chancellor, Gordon Brown *(above, with troops)* did not openly oppose the war but did not show much enthusiasm about it. Since his ascension to prime minister, Brown has assured the public the British government would reduce its military presence in Iraq.

that a suspect in Britain could be imprisoned for three months without being formally charged with a crime seemed, however, to clash with the concept of habeas corpus. Habeas corpus—the term comes from a Latin phrase meaning "you have the body"—is a writ, or summons, commanding the arresting authorities to bring a prisoner before a court. This ancient and much-venerated writ guarantees a person's right to a speedy trial. What, Blair's opponents asked, if the police decided that 90 days was not enough? Would the law then be amended to make it 900 days? Or 9,000 days? In any event, this portion of the Terrorism Act was defeated in a rebellion by Labour MPs; a shorter, 28-day maximum was introduced instead.

Since becoming prime minister, Brown has sent mixed signals about his attitude toward freedom in an age of terrorism. In October 2007, he gave a major speech on the subject. In it, he outlined a "liberty test" for all future government policies. Such policies must, he said, "respect fundamental rights and freedoms, never subject the citizen to arbitrary treatment, be transparent and proportionate, and at all times require proper scrutiny and accountability." In the same speech, he spoke of relaxing the secrecy laws that forbid access to government documents and mentioned a possible Bill of Rights and Duties for all British people. On the other hand, however, Brown has maintained his support for the introduction of a national ID card, an idea originally floated by the Blair government. Concerned opponents believe that such a card could be used to intrude on the privacy of private citizens. Brown also would like to extend the 28-day detention period allowed by the Terrorism Act.

Brown's government did itself no favors in November 2007, when it was revealed that two computer disks containing personal information about 25 million people—half the British population—had gone missing when they were sent through the mail in October. Although there has been no evidence that the disks have fallen into criminal hands (they simply may have disappeared forever), the fact that sensitive information was being handled in such a casual manner has not done much for Labour's reputation as a party that takes privacy matters seriously.

BROWN AND THE UNITED STATES

"Bush's poodle"—that was, perhaps, one of the cruelest jibes hurled against Tony Blair during his years as prime minister. Because of what has been called the "special relationship" between the two countries, the private rapport between Britain's leader and the president of the United States has been a source of interest and curiosity since World War II. Wartime prime minister Winston Churchill was half American (his mother, Jennie Jerome, was born in Brooklyn, New York) and was held in high esteem across the Atlantic. His successors often have attempted to influence United States decision making by forging personal bonds with the president of the day. In the early 1960s, Harold Macmillan was a friend and mentor of John F. Kennedy, and Margaret Thatcher was known for her staunch support of Ronald Reagan during the 1980s. In the first years of the Blair administration, it was no secret that New Labour was modeled in part on the Third Way politics of Bill Clinton's presidency, and that the Labour Party had been advised by Democratic strategists. This provoked relatively little controversy at the time. It seemed natural enough that Labour and the Democrats, as left-of-center parties, should find common ground. Additionally, Clinton was a fairly well-liked president in Britain, particularly because of his role in managing the creation of the Northern Ireland peace process.

All of that changed, however, when George W. Bush entered the White House in January 2001. From the beginning, Bush's supposedly unsophisticated approach to foreign affairs and what was called his arrogant attitude toward the rest of the world made him unpopular not only in Britain but also in the rest of Europe. It was assumed that the Labour government, which had had such a close relationship with the Clinton administration, would keep its distance from Bush. Blair discomforted many of his supporters, however, by immediately establishing a visible friendship with the new president. From the point of view of Labour stalwarts, the situation became even worse after 9/11 and the American decision to invade Iraq. Blair was almost alone among world leaders in standing by the Bush White House's policy in the Middle East. Indeed, the eloquent British prime minister often seemed to be a more effective spokesman for Bush than the president himself. Former

South African president Nelson Mandela described Blair, not very flatteringly, as "the U.S. foreign minister." Blair defended his friendship with Bush, saying that it was in Britain's vital self-interest to maintain a close harmony across the Atlantic no matter who was in control of the White House. Blair's critics, however, claimed that the Bush-Blair pact was a one-sided deal from which the United Kingdom seemed to derive very little practical benefit. The prime minister might enjoy the flattery of his American friend, but Britain gained nothing from it. In 2006, a poll suggested that 63 percent of Britons felt that their country currently was tied too closely to the United States.

When Gordon Brown succeeded Blair, there was great speculation as to how well he would get along with Bush. One of Brown's spokesmen made a rash promise that Downing Street would "no longer be joined at the hip" to the Bush administration. The prime minister quickly disassociated himself from the comment. Nonetheless, in July 2007, when Brown flew to Camp David in Maryland for his first meeting as head of government with President Bush, it was clear that although the rhetoric might be similar, the mood had changed. Blair and Bush had maintained a chummy familiarity. They dressed casually and spoke to each other in relaxed, personal terms. Brown wore a suit and kept his forms of address friendly but formal. The days when the president might greet the prime minister by yelling, "Yo, Blair!" as, famously, he once had done, were over.

The irony behind this new coolness, however, is that, if anything, Gordon Brown is probably more instinctively pro-American than Tony Blair ever was. Before his marriage, Brown used to vacation annually in Cape Cod. The Blairs preferred Italy. Brown has spent much time in the United States, and he knows the country well. His lack of enthusiasm for European integration suggests that he remains committed to the American connection. He has spoken at length about the importance of the "special relationship." In an article published in the *Washington Post*, he wrote that "I believe our Atlantic partnership is rooted in something far more fundamental and lasting than common interests or even common history: It is anchored in shared ideals that have for two centuries linked the destinies of our two countries."

If Brown seemed lukewarm towards the U.S. president during the first eighteen months of his premiership, it was probably in part because he knew that the Bush administration was heading towards its natural end. In January 2009, Barack Obama will become the forty-fourth president of the United States. A new face in Washington will offer the opportunity for a fresh start in transatlantic relations. Brown met Obama for the first time in a trip to the United States during the 2008 election campaign, and though little is known as yet about their personal rapport, the Democratic president's policy views on issues like the war on terror and climate change seem quite similar to Brown's. It is no secret that Obama was the favorite electoral candidate of most Britons in 2008, and so cozying up to the new president will represent much less of a political risk for Brown than the "special relationship" with the Republican White House did.

BROWN'S GLOBAL POLICY

Brown kept his personal feelings about Iraq quiet during his time as chancellor, and he has not admitted to any immediate second thoughts as prime minister. There is, however, some evidence that he has a rather different approach toward the problem of Middle East violence and terrorism than did Blair. Brown is said to dislike the phrase "war on terror." In his view, that phrase frames the conflict too much in terms of a crusade. He prefers to think of the conflict with al-Qaeda essentially as a criminal matter. In much the same way, the British government always refused to regard the IRA as a legitimate military opponent. This does not mean that armed force should not be used against bin Laden's followers. To position al-Qaeda's members as common criminals rather than as "evildoers" (as

President Bush once called them) is to strip them of some of their glamour. By refusing to speak of the terrorists in their own terms, the theory goes, the emotion is drained from their campaign. They become perceived more as mundane thugs than as holy warriors.

Brown also favors improving the West's image in the eyes of the rest of the world. "We must undercut the terrorists' so-called 'single narrative' and defeat their ideas," he has said. "At home and abroad," he also has said, "we must back mainstream and moderate voices and reformers, emphasizing the shared values that exist across faiths and communities." Brown has suggested that a powerful United Nations force should be deployed to war-torn Darfur in Sudan to prevent further acts of genocide against the local population. He also has strongly backed the implementation of the UN's Millennium Development Goals. These are eight targets designed to deal with poverty, illiteracy, ill health and disease, environmental degradation, and debt in the developing world. If Britain and the other countries of the developed West can show that they are serious about tackling systemic problems in Africa, Asia, and South America, their efforts (it is suggested) will undercut the appeal of radical demagogues such as bin Laden.

Hopes and Expectations

IN HIS DOCTORAL DISSERTATION ON THE LABOUR MOVEMENT IN THE 1920S, Gordon Brown wrote of James Maxton, the Scottish socialist who was regarded by no less a person than Winston Churchill as the greatest parliamentarian of his day. "He was," Brown wrote, "a politician who had every quality save one—the gift of knowing how to succeed." Could the same be said of Brown? On the face of it, the question is ridiculous. Brown has helped to lead the Labour Party to its greatest triumph in history, with three consecutive victories at general elections. As chancellor of the exchequer, he presided over one of the longest continuous periods of economic growth in recent memory. He started life as the son of an obscure Fife preacher and rose to be prime minister of Great Britain. If that is not success, what is?

But . . . Brown came to power very late. For 10 years, he had to wait in the wings as the understudy to a more charismatic and daring man. He may be prime minister now, but the legacy of the Blair years hangs over everything he does. Brown may wonder if his fate is going to be the same as that of other prime ministers who spent much of their careers overshadowed by more famous men. Anthony Eden, a handsome and dynamic young Conservative, had the misfortune of coming into office during Winston Churchill's long ascendency. For 15 frustrating years, Eden served as Churchill's loyal lieutenant. He oversaw much of the government's day-to-day business as the prime minister became older and less physically and mentally robust. Churchill stubbornly refused to make way for his deputy until ill-health finally forced him to retire in 1955. By that time, Eden was ill himself. As prime minister, he soon mishandled a crisis in the Middle East: In 1956, he sent British troops to occupy Egypt's Suez Canal Zone in defiance of American opposition. The Suez Crisis was a diplomatic disaster, and Eden had to resign after less than two years as prime minister. He now is ranked as one of the least successful prime ministers in British history. Had Churchill made way for Eden immediately after World War II, as many of his colleagues hoped he would, how much more effective might Eden's time as leader have been? One can only speculate.

CONCLUSION

Although Brown's premiership is new, New Labour is not. Labour has been in office since 1997 and it is clear that, just as Margaret Thatcher and John Major's Conservative administration eventually ran out of steam, so the voters are starting to tire of the current incumbents. True, in the first months of his government Brown enjoyed a "bounce" in the opinion polls as he unveiled a new direction for Labour; after a long period of trailing the Tories, Brown's party jumped ahead with a 13 percent lead. But his honeymoon phase did not last. By the end of 2007 the Conservatives were on top again with 40 percent of popular backing compared to 32 percent for Labour (the remaining 28 percent either undecided voters or third party supporters).

If this was an inauspicious beginning, even worse was to come in 2008. In May, in the local council elections held across England and Wales, Labour suffered its worst result in forty years when it won less than a quarter of the total vote. The same day, Labour's nominee for mayor of London lost to the Conservative candidate Boris Johnson. And in July the humiliation reached its peak when Labour lost one of its safest parliamentary seats in a special by-election in the Scottish city of Glasgow. During the summer and the fall, nervous Labour MPs began to openly grumble about the poor performance of their party's leader, some going as far as to demand his resignation. It was all eerily reminiscent of the intrigues that dogged the final years of Tony Blair's premiership.

Seeing the disarray in the government, David Cameron must be feeling increasingly confident that the Tories have finally emerged from their years in the wilderness and that they can return to power at the next general election, which Brown must call no later than 2010. Conservatives insiders have spoken of a "Blue Sky, Black Sky" strategy, comparing the young and optimistic Cameron's public face with the dour grimace of the ex-Chancellor—in other words, packaging the Tory leader much as Tony Blair was once packaged. Cameron has blasted Brown as "a creature of the past" and a robotic "speak-your-weight machine."

Certainly, Brown inherited the premiership at a difficult moment. Though the British contribution to the war in Iraq has wound down, many voters, including many former Labour supporters, have not forgotten nor forgiven Blair's administration for its perceived willingness to mislead the public. The fear that the special relationship with the United States has made Britain a greater target for terrorism persists, even in the new age of Obama; Brown and his colleagues must dread the possibility of another, perhaps even more devastating, event such as 7/7.

Labour has become associated in many people's minds with corruption and "sleaze," a taint that probably did more

Gordon Brown has pledged to take action on several controversial issues that concern the British public, like involvement in the Iraq war, climate change, and the economy. Regardless of his capabilities and promises, his future relies on the continued success of his political party and his effectiveness in office.

to destroy John Major's government than anything else. In his final year in office Blair was investigated by police—the first time this has ever happened to a sitting prime minister —when a row broke out over the alleged "sale" of aristocratic titles and other honors in return for loans to the Labour Party. The Crown Prosecution Service, which decides whether or not to formally charge alleged criminals, eventually decided that there was not enough evidence that anything technically illegal had occurred. However, Labour hardly emerged with a glowing reputation from the affair. When Tony Blair became prime minister in 1997 he had the advantage of a clean slate, and a public willing to give him the benefit of the doubt. Gordon Brown must live with the mistakes and sins of the past, many of which were not his own doing.

On the other hand, a lot could happen between this writing and Brown's reelection campaign. Although foreign policy dramas like Iraq often dominate the news headlines, there is evidence that voters ultimate choose which party to support based on "bread-and-butter" domestic issues—how well they are doing personally, and what their own expectations are for the near future. These attitudes depend crucially on the state of the economy.

At the end of 2007, Wall Street was rocked by a "credit crunch" as the sub-prime mortgage bubble burst. The effects of this crisis rippled out from New York across the world's financial markets, affecting Britain especially severely. In February 2008, Brown's government was forced to nationalize the insolvent Northern Rock bank, and in October it was announced that $37 billion in state funds would have to be invested in a group of large banks in order to prevent a looming collapse of the nation's financial system. The bailout might have helped to avert an imminent crisis, but it could do nothing to offset the grim news coming from the rest of the economy. As property prices collapsed, it was estimated that by 2009 one in six British homeowners could owe more on their mortgages than their houses were worth. Manufacturing activity declined as company bankruptcies rose. National economic growth fell to its lowest level in sixteen years. Unemployment crept up to two million at Christmas 2008.

How astutely Gordon Brown steers his country through this period of uncertainty will probably decide the fate of his government. Labour may have lost a lot of confidence across the country, but it is still seen as a party of sound economic management. That is Brown's most important feat. He is never going to be the fashionable, even loveable figure that Tony Blair once was; his peculiar personality rules that out. But then the fate of Blair suggests that people may want a break from charismatic heroes for a while. And as one journalist put it, "voters do not mind if their political leaders are a little unusual, so long as they are effective." The British public will forgive the son of the manse a great deal if he can return prosperity to the nation in challenging times.

CHRONOLOGY

1951 Gordon Brown is born in Govan, Glasgow.

1967 Enters first year at the University of Edinburgh; is soon forced to take a leave of absence because of detached retinas and spends much of the next year in hospital.

1968 Returns to Edinburgh.

1969 Joins the Labour Party.

1972 Graduates with a master of arts degree in history; elected University rector the same year; serves until 1975.

1976 Becomes a lecturer in politics at Glasgow College of Technology.

1979 Stands unsuccessfully for Parliament for the first time in that year's general election, in which Conservative leader Margaret Thatcher becomes prime minister.

1980 Becomes a journalist for Scottish Television (STV).

1982 Awarded a doctorate in history from the University of Edinburgh.

1983 Elected member of Parliament for Dunfermline East in a second general election win for Mrs. Thatcher that is otherwise disastrous for the Labour Party. Neil Kinnock becomes leader of the Labour Party.

1985 Gets his first major post as Labour spokesman for regional trade and industry affairs, working under John Smith.

1987 Mrs. Thatcher wins a third election term. Brown is appointed shadow chief secretary to the Treasury.

1989 Promoted to shadow secretary of state for trade and industry.

1990 Mrs. Thatcher resigns; she is succeeded as Conservative prime minister by John Major.

1992 John Major wins reelection for the Conservatives for a fourth consecutive time. Brown becomes Labour's shadow chancellor under the new Labour leader John Smith.

1994 John Smith dies suddenly; Tony Blair succeeds him; the birth of "New Labour."

1997 Labour is elected to power in a historic landslide victory. Brown becomes chancellor of the exchequer.

2000 Marries Sarah Macaulay.

2001 Labour is reelected for a second term. Al-Qaeda terrorists attack New York and Washington D.C.; subsequent invasion of Afghanistan by United States-led coalition. Brown's first child, Jennifer, is born but dies after less than two weeks.

2003 United States and allies invade Iraq and topple dictator Saddam Hussein.

2005 Labour is reelected for a third term. Suicide bomb attacks in London claim 52 lives.

2006 Blair announces that he will step down from office within the next 12 months.

2007 Brown becomes prime minister and leader of the Labour Party following Blair's resignation.

BIBLIOGRAPHY

Bower, Tom. *Gordon Brown.* London: HarperCollins, 2004.

Brown, Gordon. *Speeches 1997–2006.* Edited by W. Stevenson. London: Bloomsbury, 2006.

Freedland, Jonathan. "Who Is Gordon Brown?" *The New York Review of Books* 54, no. 16 (October 25, 2007).

Naughtie, James. *The Rivals: The Intimate Story of a Political Marriage.* London: Fourth Estate, 2001.

Routledge, Paul. *Gordon Brown: The Biography.* London: Simon & Schuster, 1998.

FURTHER READING

Brown, Gordon. *Britain's Everyday Heroes.* Edinburgh: Mainstream Publishing, 2007.

———. *Courage: Eight Portraits.* London: Bloomsbury, 2007.

Keegan, William. *The Prudence of Mr. Gordon Brown.* Chichester: John Wiley, 2003.

Peston, Robert. *Brown's Britain: How Gordon Runs the Show.* London: Short Books, 2005.

Rawnsley, Andrew, *Servants of the People: The Inside Story of New Labour.* London: Penguin Books, 2001.

Rosen, Greg. *Old Labour to New: The Dreams that Inspired, the Battles that Divided.* London: Politico's Publishing, 2005.

WEB SITES

10 Downing Street: The Prime Minister's Office
http://www.number10.gov.uk/

The Conservative Party
http://www.conservatives.com/

Directgov.uk: The UK's Official Government Web Site for Citizens
http://www.direct.gov.uk/en/index.htm

The Labour Party
http://www.labour.org.uk/home

United Kingdom Parliament
http://www.parliament.uk/

PHOTO CREDITS

page:

3: Associated Press
14: © Matthew Polak/Sygma/
CORBIS
16: Associated Press
23: © Chris Malcolm
28: University of Edinburgh special collections
34: Associated Press
45: © Adam_Butler/PA-FILES/
epa/CORBIS
50: Associated Press
54: © POOL/Reuters/CORBIS
60: © DAN CHUNG/Reuters/
CORBIS
64: Associated Press
69: Associated Press
74: © Raoul Dixon/epa/CORBIS
77: Associated Press
83: Assoociated Press
87: Associated Press
93: Associated Press
99: Associated Press
108: © Lipin Garcia/epa/
CORBIS

INDEX

About the Authors

ALAN ALLPORT was born in Whiston, England, and grew up in East Yorkshire. He has a doctorate in history from the University of Pennsylvania and is currently a lecturer at Princeton University. He is the author of *American Military Policy*, *Freedom of Speech*, and *Immigration Policy, Second Edition* in Chelsea House's Point/Counterpoint series.

ARTHUR SCHLESINGER, JR. is remembered as the leading American historian of our time. He won the Pulitzer Prize for his books *The Age of Jackson* (1945) and *A Thousand Days* (1965), which also won the National Book Award. Schlesinger was the Albert Schweitzer Professor of the Humanities at the City University of New York and was involved in several other Chelsea House projects, including the series *Revolutionary War Leaders*, *Colonial Leaders*, and *Your Government*.